We-Topia

How Ego Broke the World and How We Can Fix It

Previous Books

Provolution: A Guide to Changing the World Through Personal Evolution
ISBN: 978-1-84694-310-2

Equanimous: A Channeled Dialog of The Past, Present and Future of Humanity
ISBN: 978-1-7396007-0-9

Why on Earth Are You Here? A Guide to Your Life's Spiritual Purpose on Earth
ISBN: 978-1-7396007-1-6

We-Topia

How Ego Broke the World and How We Can Fix It

Michael Paul Stephens

BOOKS

Winchester, UK
Washington, USA

JOHN HUNT PUBLISHING

First published by O-Books, 2023
O-Books is an imprint of John Hunt Publishing Ltd., 3 East St., Alresford,
Hampshire SO24 9EE, UK
office@jhpbooks.com
www.johnhuntpublishing.com
www.o-books.com

For distributor details and how to order please visit the 'Ordering' section on our website.

Text copyright: Michael Paul Stephens 2022

ISBN: 978 1 80341 238 2
978 1 80341 239 9 (ebook)
Library of Congress Control Number: 2022937919

A CIP catalogue record for this book is available from the British Library.

Design: Lapiz Digital

UK: Printed and bound by CPI Group (UK) Ltd, Croydon, CR0 4YY
Printed in North America by CPI GPS partners

The author of this book does not dispense medical advice or
prescribe the use of any technique as a form of treatment for
physical, emotional, or medical problems without the advice of a
physician, either directly or indirectly. The intent of the author
is only to offer information of a general nature to help you in
your quest for emotional and spiritual well-being. In the event
you use any of the information in this book for yourself, which is
your constitutional right, the author and the publisher assume no
responsibility for your actions.

We operate a distinctive and ethical publishing philosophy in
all areas of our business, from our global network of authors to
production and worldwide distribution.

Contents

For Buddhadasa and all those who never give up

Introduction

Can the world change? Can we create an inclusive place, where equality reigns and everyone is at liberty to pursue their life goals? Answering this question has been a dream of mine. And this book is my attempt to realize it.

I've long been interested in how Buddhist philosophy and practice answer those tough questions. I perceive Buddhism, not from a religious viewpoint, but as a profound set of ideas that get great results in the real world. In fact, at their heart, Buddha's teachings are what you might call 'anti-religious' because he didn't ask us to accept on faith a single speck of what he taught. Indeed, Buddha explicitly asked us to challenge his ideas. And that's about as brave as any teaching can be. It says, "Try this!" And: "Throw every single question at it that you can!" The madness of this idea, simply put, is that a truthful set of ideas will stand up to scrutiny and work for you. There will never be a need for faith if good results are tangible in your life. We-Topia takes this idea and applies it to our modern society. A good, healthy society will withstand scrutiny and criticism. But an insecure, superficial one will balk and shoot the messenger.

It is therefore appropriate that the works of one of Thailand's great Buddhists, the Venerable Ajarn Buddhadasa Bhikkhu, inspires *We-Topia*. Between the 1930s and 1990s, his revisionist interpretation of the Buddha's teachings challenged the conventional views of the clergy and laypeople alike but, like any iconoclast, Buddhadasa faced the broad shoulders of conservative inertia as he stepped foot on that thorny path!

However, Buddhadasa knew that Buddhism needs a spring clean every so often. The Buddha lived over 2500 years ago and, over such a long stretch of history, any philosophy can succumb to mysticism and superstition. Buddhadasa's objective was not to laud his own ideas but to simply dust off some of the accumulated detritus and return Buddha's teaching to its most practical, accessible roots. He wanted to show Buddhism in its most coherent form: an accessible tool to deal with life's problems, a resource for the pursuit of happiness.

So, in 1931, in his hometown of Chaiya, Buddhadasa established his forest temple, Suan Mokkh, meaning 'Garden of Liberation.' There, he began offering retreats to both Thais and international students in the study and practice of Buddha-Dhamma.[1] Since then, his talks and writings have been celebrated all over the world as a great contribution to Buddhism and world peace. In 2006, to celebrate the one hundredth anniversary of his birth, he was recognized by UNESCO as one of the Truly Great Personalities of the World. In this iconoclastic spirit, it is therefore appropriate, not only that Buddha-Dhamma is the lens through which I approach We-Topia, but also that Buddhadasa is my guide for the journey.

One of the most attractive qualities of Buddha-Dhamma is its unrivaled ability to demonstrate, with astounding clarity, how the human mind is the root cause of all our problems, a point eloquently made by Buddhadasa in his book *Dhammic Socialism*. This constructive application of Buddha-Dhamma to social problems ignited my interest in social philosophy and a search to find the answer to how we can all live together without killing each other *or* the planet.

What struck me upon reading *Dhammic Socialism* was the clear correlation between an incomplete understanding of 'reality' and the social problems that creates. Issues like inequality, ecological destruction, and ingrained social stratification are not just bad choices acted out with awful consequences. They begin as *mental imbalances*. The minds in which these choices begin are simply unaware of what is real and what is simply a figment of their imagination. This creates bias and selfishness in people's actions. And if the mind is the source of this output, then all negative outcomes in society have psychological remedies.

I began to wonder if this same mental imbalance was evident in history and so I applied Buddha-Dhamma to humanity's legacy, asking the questions of how and why our collective past has resulted in today's materialistic society, so apathetic to the needs of the planet. If I applied the basic tenets of Buddha-Dhamma to the story of human evolution and development from the nomadic society to the modern digital society, what might it reveal about the true roots of our social issues and how to repair them?

The result is this book: *We-Topia*. And what I found was shocking to me.

I traveled back through history to discover that much of what I had been taught in history classes at school can best be described as wild assumptions and suppositions. When I began, I assumed that history was a long unimpeded journey towards progress, *human evolution*, and a more successful, happier society. Doesn't everyone assume that? So it must be true, right?

But what I found was not a path of development at all, but a paradigm of confusion and illusions creeping across history that has hidden a higher pathway of potential from us all. So much of what we assume to be true about history is bogus. In fact, in the most crucial ways, our ancient ancestors may have been happier, healthier, and more spiritually conscious than all of us!

But the most shocking realization of all was concerning the state of this world we have fashioned from the best choices of our collective consciousness. In a time when every opinion is fact-checked, Siri can instantly quote any encyclopedia in the world, and debate forums across a million websites challenge every assumption with zeal, I made a startling discovery: the whole society of humankind is founded on a lie. And not just a small one. A *global* one.

We have somehow contrived to manufacture a reality that not only completely and utterly misunderstands the *real* needs of human beings, but has also perverted the course of human history away from our highest potential. We have regressed from egalitarian, spiritual societies where people forsake possessions and nurture each other, into an ego-led fiction that perpetuates human misery, hoards resources, and works best for the benefit of a few at the expense of our entire species' evolution.

In 1516, Sir Thomas More coined the word 'Utopia' in the title of his book, a term that represented a fictional idyllic society. It was a pun on two Greek words that together meant 'no-place.' More wasn't referring to either a future or a past iteration of a perfect society, but to an unattainable perfection forever beyond our reach.

With this definition ringing in my mind, I wrote *We-Topia*. I believe that Utopia is the unattainable goal we are *already* seeking: a world where we will make ourselves healthier and better by consuming more and caring less. This is the truest illusion going and, amid this illusion, I riff on More's title, in full agreement with his assertion that a perfect society is a dream most worthy of a pun or three, and probably a good kick up its idealistic backside too!

But that doesn't mean we can't do better. At the very *least* we should all expect from society a place where people are treated equally, valued equally, and taught the most basic skills and concepts to engender happiness in their life. That shouldn't be too much to ask, should it?

But here we are, living together in a world that not only fails to attain such an average ambition but also fails while destroying the planet and each other simultaneously. Thus, the purpose of *We-Topia* is not idealism in any shape or form. It expects no miracles or epiphanies. *We-Topia* is a pragmatic investigation into why we live the way we do and what we gave up to live this way. Moreover, it asks you whether you are ready to stop embracing the misconceptions of our past, the lies about our future, and the illusions we have all been taught to believe are real.

Simply put, *We-Topia* is a journey from 'me' to 'we.' And you don't even have to set foot off your sofa.

Chapter 1

The Purest Natural Socialism

When Buddhadasa first presented the core ideas of *Dhammic Socialism*, his book landed on the conservative coffee tables of Bangkok's elite with a percussive thud. He wouldn't have been surprised by its reception. It was published in 1973; the country was embroiled in revolution; a bloody uprising by left-wing students had just toppled Thailand's military dictatorship. Some perceived *Dhammic Socialism* as more grist for the mill of chaos.

It's all about context. The 1970s were a time when domino theory was the greatest fear of the global political elite. Thailand was a US base for its secret war in Laos, and the Communist insurgency in the north of the country stoked fears that Thailand was about to crumble under the 'Red Threat.' In this mayhem, Buddhadasa's book was widely misunderstood as something of a Commie manifesto, an outrageous overreach from one of the most celebrated members of the supposedly non-political *sangha*, the Buddhist community.

Yet, this concern was founded on many misconceptions. The title of his book was not proposing *political* 'Socialism' at all. Buddhadasa was merely doing his job by discussing how the principles of Buddha-Dhamma might be applied to Thai society. In a sense, it was something of a thought experiment, asking the question: how might society be organized if it pursued higher consciousness rather than higher technology? After all, the problems of the era were not products of wisdom. No one perceives bloody war or political violence as the finest output of our intellectual prowess. Everyone recognized that the world was spiraling into more suffering and that there had to be another way. Buddhadasa wasn't about to sit around and

7

do nothing when he had been practicing an alternative virtually his whole life.

Moreover, Buddhadasa was no Luddite. He believed higher consciousness and better technology could be partners in society if we applied nature's creative principles to society rather than humankind's destructive principles to nature. The problem he encountered was that the word 'socialism' held many negative connotations, as it still does today. It's equated with Marxism, Stalin or Mao, the Cold War, gulags and totalitarianism, and so on. But he wasn't stupid. He *knew* that. And named his book to get a response.

The fact is, Buddhadasa had a very different interpretation of the word 'socialism.' He viewed conventional political socialism with no less dismay than the current social system, which he called Capitalist Liberal Democracy (CLD). And he said as much:

> Groups act against the harmony of nature, or the good of the whole, one from its position of financial power, the other from the power of its labor. The confrontation threatens mutual destruction. This sort of violent, bloody socialism arises from excessive selfishness which does not consider others' right to live in the same world. The division of human beings into different groups at enmity with one another is neither the purpose of nature (dhammajati) nor any religion.[1]

Buddhadasa recognized that no political ideology, left or right, had been effective at building a tolerant and fair society, despite each portraying itself as a panacea for all ills. None had offered any *real* solutions to society's problems and both engaged in the endless pursuit of political power. Perhaps Buddhadasa was reminded of John Kenneth Galbraith's quip, when the American economist, public official, and diplomat said: "Under capitalism, man exploits man. Under communism, it's just the opposite."

So, why did Buddhadasa choose to use the word 'socialism' at all? Well, to answer this question, we need to understand why Buddhadasa built his celebrated temple and retreat center, Suan Mokkh, among the forests of Chaiya in southern Thailand. On this matter, he said:

As we sit here in this forest, surrounded by nature, we feel the calming effects of the natural environment. "Socialist" thoughts and feelings arise from such a calm state—socialist in the most profound sense of the truth of Nature. Here, we are not under the influence of a violent worldly socialism so our minds can remain undisturbed, allowing us to see and participate in the natural balance that pervades everything— earth, water, air, fire, and consciousness—the internal and external aspects of everything. Here is true socialism—the embodiment of Nature in a pure, balanced state. Here there is no deceit, no "me/mine" distinctions; they simply do not exist.[2]

So, Buddhadasa's Dhammic 'socialism' does not hail from a political ideology at all. Its origin is the cohesive reality of nature, the same reality that resides within you and me. Nature favors no political system, nor holds any bias for one species or another. It is neither conservative nor liberal, neither left nor right. It is fair, consistent, and universal. Most of all, natural systems offer us profound guidance towards a better way of living:

Nothing in Nature exists independently; no creature, element, or molecule can exist by itself. All aspects of Nature combine in an interdependent relationship. Even an atom is a socialistic system of interdependent parts. A molecule also exhibits socialistic characteristics in that it is made up of several interdependent atoms. On and on it goes—molecules combine to form tissue, tissues combine to form flesh or leaves or whatever, all interdependent and in balance, according to the principles of Nature's pure socialism.[3]

Buddhadasa's interpretation of socialism was founded upon his perspective of interdependence. Just as he saw the interdependence of everything in every natural system, so too did he see the interdependence of all people in a society. From atoms to molecules, to cells, to entire bodies, and the social systems that organize those bodies into human culture, the natural patterns of interdependence form the structure of the systems that govern everything. It was only, well, *natural* that he would conclude these same natural patterns as being the best ones by which to govern ourselves.

And yet, society didn't seem to agree with his viewpoint. What he saw around the world in the 1970s and 1980s was conflict, often deliberately being promulgated and stoked between diverse interests. In that respect, Buddhadasa's world was no different from the twenty-first century. We had not then, nor have we ever since, been able to find an inclusive way to respect differences, tolerate diversity, or bridge the gap between our selfish interests and the interests of other people in the world around us.

Indeed, this problem seems to have deepened. Today, the world encourages us to divide into smaller and smaller groups fighting for our share, afraid we will lose out. We act at odds with our natural urge to unite and support one another. Our fears swell as we distrust other people's motives and ambitions. It seems that we do not live in a world getting better but a world whose sickness is burrowing deeper into our psyches, isolating us in our homes and communities, separating us into smaller groups, magnifying our frustrations, and highlighting our differences.

Yet, the question that formed in Buddhadasa's mind during the 1970s was surely the same one that sparked in my mind before I sat down to write *We-Topia*. If the entire universe is an interdependent and cooperative system, and we have known this for many, many years, why do our societies fail to engender anything like this same level of unity? They almost seem to *revel* in disunity! In short, *why* have we failed, for thousands of years, to create a society that respects nature's pure socialism and seeks to fulfill the needs of us all?

Why, indeed.

Chapter 2

A Society of Winners and Losers

Buddhadasa believed: "All aspects of Nature combine in an interdependent relationship." This was no metaphor. It was not his ideological position. It is a fact supported by the chemical, biological, and physical sciences. Go check Wikipedia. I did.

At the cellular level, each of us is composed of billions and billions of cellular examples of this very interdependence. Every living creature and the entire planet is the *ultimate* example of a society in which each life form, cell, or atom is but an interconnected piece.

Most profoundly, from this fact, we can also deduce that there is a profound commonality between all life forms on the Earth. *Every* living being struggles, suffers, and desires to achieve their definition of comfort and happiness, just like you and me. Fish, trees, birds, insects, plants: all sentient life wants to be safe, secure, fed, watered, comforted, and without suffering, sickness, or fear.

There are two ways we can respond to this understanding of interdependence. We can either respect it and *cooperate* or reject it and *compete*. Both choices have far-reaching implications for human society and the natural world beyond. Imagine, for example, if the cells of your body suddenly rejected interdependence and stopped cooperating. As they competed for resources with one another, you would soon be destroyed from the inside. So why would we assume that these larger aggregations of cells (*human society*) can survive by favoring competitive independence too?

Recognizing that the personal desire for independence can lead to mutual destruction, society should be at pains to cultivate a healthier balance between the competitive individual and the collective needs of the community. Stimulating trust, equality, and fairness attains this. It's not a secret formula. You'll not be surprised by it any more than I am. It's about cultivating all those lovely interdependent attitudes in people that build closer bonds of community and cooperation. We can't do this in isolation from one another. When we feel respected by others—safe, secure, and valued in a group—we reflect bonds of empathy and collaboration that unite society as one. It is symbiotic, just like nature. That's clear. But, when this delicate balance between competition and cooperation tips in favor of competition, social values begin to erode and friction in the community emerges.

So how effective is CLD at building the bonds of trust, equality, and fairness that unite society? Well, let's answer that question with a quick statistical review of life in the twenty-first century in that bastion of CLD, the United States of America:

- In 2021, the top 1% of American society possessed 27% of the country's total wealth, which is more than the entire middle class combined.[1]
- In the same year, the bottom 20% accounted for just 2% of this total.[2]
- According to the Pew Research Institute: "The wealth gap between America's richest and poorer families more than doubled from 1989 to 2016."[3]
- In 2020, over 580,000 Americans (equivalent to the population of Copenhagen) were homeless and nearly 230,000 of them slept on the streets. That's approximately 1 in 588 Americans without a home.[4]
- 50% of US adults were found to be unable to read an eighth-grade level book.[5]
- 66% of all Americans in 2019 were prescribed some kind of pharmaceutical remedy for health issues.[6]
- In 2019, 19.2% of adults received mental health treatment. That's over 62 million people![7]

- The Pew Research Center claims that "The difference in median household incomes between white and black Americans has grown from about $23,800 in 1970 to roughly $33,000 in 2018 (as measured in 2018 dollars)."[8]
- The current global extinction rate is 1000 times the natural level and this level is predicted to rise to ten times that rate soon.[9]
- Our consumption of natural resources is accelerating at such a speed that, by 2030, it is predicted we will need two planets to sustain our global economy.[10]

I'm not picking on the United States of America. And these statistics are not cherry-picked. I use the USA as my example because it is acknowledged as one of the world's foremost advocates of the Capitalist Liberal Democratic model for society. And, as is evident, the truth is damning. CLD is anything but social. Enormous social disunity, inequality, and ecological chaos should not exist if you are *designing* a country to *be social*. But it does exist. I mean, I apologize if I am stating the obvious and I find myself somewhat ashamed to have to even state this, but it seems that I do: no *healthy* and *functioning* social system should have to treat nearly a fifth of its population for mental health issues each year. *Something* is clearly wrong. Not just with the USA, but with the paradigm that has built and sustains the systems of the entire world today.

What's wrong is our unhealthy obsession with competition. Many might argue that competition is a natural system too, but in nature, competitive systems harmonize with their interdependent whole. They are situational, occasional, and contextual. They maintain a subtle presence in an otherwise interdependent natural system that ensures *all* creatures have enough space, resources, and opportunity to thrive.

However, in the case of humanity, there is no argument that we are social beings and that we exist in an interdependent natural environment. Yet, winning a global competition against each other and dominating all other species on the Earth seems to have been our mission! We have rarely cooperated with nature. Subdued it, possessed it, blasted it, exploited it, killed it, and controlled it: *yes!* But cooperated: not so much. This mentality is but a stark symptom of a mental imbalance that has come about, not because you and I, the ordinary people of this planet, want *enough* to survive. It is the result of some people, groups, corporations, or countries that insist upon having *more than their fair share*. They have fixated their minds on monopolizing global resources, which in turn unbalances the ecology of the planet, ignoring the needs of other species.

Why does humanity insist on competing when, in an interdependent natural system, if we are consistently creating losers, the winners will obviously lose out too at some point? It's myopic madness to assume that just because you are winning today, the blowback from that victory won't get you tomorrow! And this myopia deepens our sense of separation from nature; it fuels a mentality of selfish immediacy and has resulted in a catastrophic competitive global policy wherein the entire web of life has been pushed to the brink of collapse.

Do we see the competition between the tree and the chainsaw as being fair? Maybe we do. As we see from the statistics cited above, the game of social competition between rich and poor is loaded just as unfairly and we're cool with that. In society, your hundred dollars and mine must compete for resources against another guy with a billion dollars. And yet we're conditioned to accept that that is the way things must be. The truth of the matter is that both the battle for ecological supremacy on our planet and economic hierarchy in our society is the same battle repeated: a war of *control*, a war of *power*, a war of *selfishness*.

Here's the deal: CLD does not seek harmony. Its system is rigged to ensure the winners keep winning and the losers keep losing. Even though we can statistically show that competition has the lowest number of advantages for the highest proportion of people, our wisest economists, politicians, and corporate leaders still persevere with it. Imagine if your own body made such a choice. What if your legs were favored over your arms? Or your lungs were considered less deserving of resources than your kidneys? You would be mad to choose such a method of determining which parts of your body deserve nutrients! How long would it be before you became diseased and died?

The fiction that prevails in the world is that CLD is the most humane social system ever devised. But for reasons that will become clear as we progress through *We-Topia*, I wholeheartedly disagree with this notion. Indeed, we have chosen to adopt the most extreme form of Darwin's 'survival of the fittest' mantra, misinterpreting it as a doctrine of war against nature and each other. This pervasive, insidious ideology has nudged society towards unhealthy competitive policies that view compassion and fairness as weaknesses. The systems are *designed* to manufacture inequality so that the fittest must fight to rise to the top. Society has become like some global Roman Colosseum and in this brutal paradigm, normalized across the world, wealth and resources are the criteria of fitness. At the heart of CLD is a value system that has corrupted the very essence of what it means to be human.

Just spend a few moments carefully digesting this quote by Adam Smith, one of the founders of Capitalist thought, and you'll see that, even 500 years ago, he knew very well society's true direction of travel!

The rich, in particular, are necessarily interested to support that order of things which can alone secure them in the possession of their own advantages. Men of inferior wealth combine to defend those of superior wealth in the possession of their property, in order that men of superior wealth may combine to defend them in the possession of theirs. All the inferior shepherds and herdsmen feel that the security of their own herds and flocks depends upon the security of those of the great shepherd or herdsman; that the maintenance of their lesser authority depends upon that of his greater authority, and that upon their subordination to him depends his power of keeping their inferiors in subordination to them...Civil government, so far as it is instituted for the security of property, is in reality instituted for the defence of the rich against the poor, or of those who have some property against those who have none at all.[11]

And therein lies the most corrosive truth of CLD. It is a delivery system to legitimize unfair competition, overemphasizing its value to the point where society itself is harmed, sometimes to the point where it ceases to be truly social. It sorts us into groups of winners and losers, rich and poor, safe and struggling, powerful and powerless, until it becomes less of a social unit and more a collection of disparate groups seeking independence from other groups they no longer trust.

Weren't we all taught that 'all men are created equal'? That's not just a nice idea. It's nature's way. We're all given a body, a mind, and a spirit with which to experience this life and explore the world. Our equality is not a philosophical ideal. It is the natural order of the Earth, an order that only humankind would have the hubris to depose.

Yet, in how many countries does CLD ignore this natural order so that some niche group can assert competitive dominance? Whether in despotic regimes, insular kingdoms, or any iteration of CLD's class systems, human equality is conveniently ignored in favor of some fabricated status. Wealth, historical hierarchy, racial dominance, religious supremacy, gender bias: each of these artificial constructs is a common rationalization, trotted out to explain why the ambitions of human beings should trump the laws of this universe.

Gandhi said, "I object to violence because when it appears to do good, the good is only temporary; the evil it does is permanent." This idea, when applied to Capitalist Liberal Democracy, perfectly reflects its fundamental failings as a social system. Yes, it has appeared to do some good: global GDP (gross domestic product) has skyrocketed; general poverty is in decline; disease is being eradicated, and so on. There are fine achievements that cannot be denied. But it also should be acknowledged that it achieves this goal through immense violence, at a huge mental and spiritual cost, and by cutting a swathe through the very social fabric it is supposed to be stitching together.

John Maynard Keynes, the founder of modern macroeconomics, had a keen mind for identifying the false assumption within the economic premise of CLD. He said: "Capitalism is the astounding belief that the most wickedest of men will do the most wickedest of things for the greatest good of everyone." This pithy quip perfectly captures why the biggest problem with CLD is the very reason it succeeds: it taps into the worst excesses of the human ego: *selfishness and greed*.

This is no small matter. We may laugh off the obvious outrage that CLD society gleans its power by pandering to our greedy desires, but this is a far more serious accusation than all the rest put together. The fact that we do not recognize it is just one more symptom of the highly effective social conditioning by which our outrage is subdued. We are indoctrinated to fear some illusions but to also trust the things that should terrify us.

Indeed, since prehistoric times our wisest spiritual sages have warned us to cork the human ego like a genie in a bottle. They have consistently sounded the alarm that our innermost demons have the potential to escape, run riot, and destroy us all. How many times do we need to hear the message that the human mind is a sucker for being tricked into believing its enemy is its friend before we look back and wonder, "Did we trust in a *lie*?" The story of 'The Wolf in Sheep's Clothing' was no biblical fable. It was a warning ignored.

Be under no illusions, CLD *systemizes* social stratification. It *needs* it. It *embraces* it. By color, age, creed, sex, size, or whatever category is needed to differentiate us, competitive social systems always promote some people and demote others. Sometimes it's subtle; sometimes it's not. Sometimes it's slight; sometimes it's like a sledgehammer to the guts. Either way, the evidence is compelling. CLD proliferates social hierarchies, fragmentation, and polarization to the point where it eventuates in apartheid by wealth, by race, by opportunity, by potential, even by hope!

Maynard Keynes and Gandhi both pointedly pondered the question of a system's social value if, by its application, we are all slowly divided by it. What good is a social system that slowly erodes society? And this is exactly the effect of CLD. Let me be even clearer: I am suggesting that Capitalist Liberal Democracy is *not a real social system at all*. It appears to be. Many of us live quietly within it. But it fails the fit-for-purpose test. Were we assessing it as a duck, it would fail to quack, waddle, or fly south for the winter.

In reality, and as this book will show in great detail, CLD is a facade, an increasingly sophisticated illusion manufactured over millennia by the ego, as an extension of its control and power. It holds individual choice as sovereign, rationalizing the devastating impact of personal greed on families and communities as either an idiosyncrasy or their own fault. "There's no rigged dice at this casino," so we're told. But we're told this by The Man, who is also well aware that hundreds of thousands of people in the wealthiest country in the world sleep on his streets each winter. How much longer do we trust the people who have the power to change that but, instead of changing the system, blame the homeless for being homeless?

When you consider the facts, in a system where the individual's right to compete to become a multibillionaire is valued above many other people's right to life itself, there are billions of rigged dice hiding in plain sight. What else can be deduced from a system that not only perpetuates class and racial inequality but also seems to *require it* for both a cheap labor resource and as a constant threat of the painful demise that awaits the unruly? For what other purpose would a system *build in* social stratification than to facilitate the exploitation of one set of people by another? That is in no way social. It is manipulative, abusive, and, if one uses Gandhi's term, it supports an evil that is permanent, for it existed as a facet of the human character for as long as humanity has existed on our Earth.

Chapter 3

The Purpose of Life

So what?

What does it matter whether CLD is excessively competitive? It may not be absolutely fair. It may not even promote equality. But it's the best system we've got. It makes us *strong*. It rewards the hardest workers. What are your alternatives? Communism? Utopia is a wishy-washy dream and anything better than CLD is romantic idealism from a fantasy world!

These are the kinds of arguments I hear regularly bandied around when CLD is challenged. But they all miss the point. What I contemplate when assessing the merits of CLD as a social system is not just whether it divides wealth effectively, provides homes, treats people fairly, or has a structure that nurtures social connectivity. These should be the non-negotiable output of *any* effective social system. So, a failure in these categories is a symptom of an even *more* critical fault. We cannot change the products of society when it is predicated on faith in competition because we cannot change the output of a competition. To evolve from a system of dividing people into winners and losers, we first need to change the system's purpose.

Now, this is going to sound a little ridiculous, but my primary concern with CLD is that it doesn't answer *the purpose of life*. Yes, I know it sounds like criticizing paracetamol for not curing cancer. And, in the case of an entire social system, it's fair to assume that most people believe that a) the purpose of life is an impossible question to answer, and b) society *can't* achieve that even if it was possible to answer!

Fair enough. But let's put those objections aside for a moment (we will come back to them) and pose a number of key questions. What is a society for? *Why* are we being social in the first place? Why do human beings feel the need to live together? Is it just for security? For companionship? Just for laughs? What is the point of banding together, being communal, sharing, and creating a society unless there is some *deeper benefit* in doing so?

Whether we are conscious of it or not, all societies are busy answering the question of life's purpose. We just don't call it that. Some have a Constitution or a Bill of Rights and they make a big palaver about these documents because they *are* a big palaver. They matter. They're why we are in this together! They're what a group of people stands for! But there has never been a Bill of Rights or a Constitution that specifically incorporates *the meaning of life* into its text, right? Because it's an impossible question to answer. After all, if the answer were known, wouldn't you have been taught it in school? Wouldn't it be front and center of every educational curriculum in every country in the world?

Right?

Right?

But what if it wasn't an impossible question at all? What if the answer to life's purpose has been known for thousands of years but has simply been ignored? And, what if the reason why we all ignore the answer today is because we have been deliberately taught to focus our minds on other things? CLD not only fails to respect the principles of nature that support an equal society but, what if, for *millennia*, it has *designed* society to teach its citizens social values that slowly erode the spiritual purpose of humanity?

That's a couple of massive claims right there: the answer to the meaning of life is known and society has been deliberately hiding it from its population! Wow! And a few paragraphs below, I will share with you a passage from Buddhadasa's teachings that explains why I believe those claims to be totally accurate. But if you're skeptical, great! In fact, Buddhadasa was the ultimate skeptic. He felt so skeptical about every idea

Buddha taught that he took Buddha's ideas and theories and, through personal practice, worked diligently to establish for himself whether they were true or not. Only then could he utterly agree with them. Moreover, you can do the same with this book. There is nothing in here that you cannot check for yourself and there's nothing that you should accept without checking.

But for the time being, I want to cover the conclusions that Buddhadasa came to regarding life's purpose. It all boils down to the biggest idea of them all—God. Now, I know that the 'G-word' has the potential to turn off both ends of the belief spectrum, but before you cancel me and retreat to your atheistic/ evangelical bunker in California/Tennessee, let me explain what I mean by bandying around the 'G-word' without fair warning!

Buddhadasa didn't ascribe to the Abrahamic idea of a sky god but likened God to the natural laws that govern all things. We had a taste of that in the last chapter on interdependence. But he also insisted that in nature's laws we find the answer to the greatest riddle humankind will ever face, *life's meaning*, and when we sit down, still our thoughts, and observe nature working right there in the midst of our mind, the illusions we have embraced as reality begin to fall away and life's deepest purpose is revealed.

When you analyze that technique objectively, it sounds a lot like how science works, doesn't it? One person experiments and then other people check the same process to see if they get the same results. The difference here is that this technique is subjective and spiritual, not objective and rational. The results are a transformation in feelings of oneness, unity, compassion and *empathy*. Then, when faced with a choice between ideas like competition and cooperation, it becomes not so much a matter of an intellectual selection or asking, "What's in it for me?", but more about *choosing to move towards the unity that you found in your practice.*

Buddhadasa found what Buddha found. What you *feel* is real. And when you truly understand what a society is, you'll realize it only works for everyone if each of us *feels* our connection to it working for us personally. Anything else is a sham.

For thousands of years, it has been known that an intense study of your mind will reveal the ultimate truth of nature to you. Indeed, your personal ability to realize this remarkable potential is the best-kept secret on Earth. This secret world, in this secret place, has the power to unite humanity together into a single tribe that transcends the petty divisions of genders, races, tax brackets, and faiths.

However, this is more than just a set of nice ideas that sounds fluffy and warm on paper. It is a real process that anyone can learn. Moreover, the results are extraordinary. This is what Buddhadasa said about it:

There is really only one society in the world: the community of humankind. We must collectively attempt to overcome our common problem, *dukkha*, by doing whatever will bring us to a fuller understanding of the term *Dhamma* or God in its most profound sense.[1]
(my emphasis)

Buddhadasa made no bones about it: life's spiritual purpose is to overcome *dukkha*. And we do this by understanding *Dhamma*, which, says Buddhadasa, *is God*. These two words, Dhamma and dukkha, are incredibly important concepts to bear in mind as we move forward through *We-Topia*. Let's explore dukkha first and then cover Dhamma more deeply in later parts of the book.

Dukkha, says Buddhadasa, is the common problem of humanity. It is a word from the Pali language of ancient India and is normally translated as 'suffering.' When I use the word 'suffering,' your mind may conjure up images of great physical pain or sickness, but this is only its crudest meaning. In truth, dukkha refers to myriad forms of subtle suffering that arise in the mind, body, and spirit. It is quite mundane and normal, like a dull hum of *unsatisfactoriness* that you will feel at some point every day of your life, and is triggered by myriad causes such as:

Mental and physical craving: Dukkha can often take several forms in one experience. For example, when you wake up in the morning and need a coffee, you feel both physical and mental dukkha. Your body feels tired and your mind wants its fix, both at the same time. These feelings won't go away (you may even get a headache) until they are sated. That's subtle dukkha, right there.

Spiritual self-loathing: A poor self-image. Maybe you have learned to be negative about yourself. This is a long-term creation of feelings that engender powerlessness, inadequacy, and self-loathing: examples of dukkha manifested over a lifetime of beliefs and expectations.

Mental anguish: This can take many different forms. Sadness for a lost relative, fear of a future event, frustration when driving, and so on. Each form of dukkha begins in the mind and affects the body (causing tension, crying, etc.). Very often, we're already in this mode without even knowing it has crept up on us. Dukkha can be very hard to avoid when you do not even feel it coming!

Physical pain: Then, there are the more obvious kinds of physical dukkha such as a toothache, stubbing your toe, or breaking a bone. These are often gross sensations that seem to have a fixed starting point, like the start of a toothache. But they can also have roots in a multitude of past events culminating in the present powerful feeling. Naturally, you want to get rid of them as quickly as you can!

This short list is just a rough guide to the multitude of forms in which you'll feel dukkha. I don't want to give the impression that it is a special feeling or experience. On the contrary, it is a common, ongoing phenomenon rooted in feelings that can arise and fall from many different sources, sometimes simultaneously! While it is fair to say that suffering is with us every day of our lives, this is not as depressing to consider as it first sounds! In fact, recognizing dukkha in our mind and using it for our benefit is an *incredibly* important factor in determining whether you will answer the question of life's purpose or whether you become a powerless victim of it.

Sadly, few of us are taught to observe dukkha in action. It is a practice pigeonholed into the weird world of religious sects and spiritual gurus rather being perceived for what it really is: a simple exercise of the mind, essential to the wellbeing of us all. So, believing that such a practice is extreme, we fail to deal with these feelings, and brush them off as common vexations, the slings and arrows of everyday life. CLD has conditioned us to suppress these *negative* feelings or obscure them with delightful experiences, moving on without a second thought, never realizing that these feelings are *not inevitable*. They are your *creations* and symptomize that what you are creating for yourself is not what you really need to be happy. When studied, these feelings can reveal the answer to life's greatest mystery: the human condition. As the saying goes, pain is inevitable, but suffering is a choice. It's true. But when were you ever taught the simple skill of taking a moment to stop and choose what you do with your feelings? Never. But you probably learned what quadratic equations are: now that's essential life-knowledge.

Every day of your life and all day long you race through events of various emotional magnitude because you have trained your mind to *cope* with your reality, not to be conscious of or even *change* its root causes. We're all living under this false premise that, to phrase it in common parlance, 'shit happens!' We all have problems. They're inevitable, which is also true. But *how* we deal with those situations, and whether we repeat them incessantly, is not inevitable at all. It is a matter of how your mind has been conditioned: to react and respond without thinking, or to choose an option that respects the reality of dukkha and Dhamma.

Ultimately, CLD conditions us all to react to our feelings and respond through patterns of behavior that do not address the root causes of our suffering but suppress their spiritual, emotional, and mental causes. Frequently, this only deepens those causes. We ignore emotional issues, coach ourselves to get through mental stresses, and hang our hats on acquiring more materials as a solution for all discomfort. And while material change *looks* like progress, it's not. In fact, you could call it immaterial, if you liked a rubbish pun.

Few of us have learned to let situations go. We dwell on small matters. We complain about them. They go around and around in our heads. And they affect us all day long. The *frustration* of a mislaid earphone, the *anger* of facing a dodgy driver on the road, the *fear* of losing your job, the *sadness* of a breakup, the physical *pain* of stubbing your toe, the *angst* of whether you are good enough, the *hope* of getting your heart's desires, the *loss* of love, the *elation* of success, and so on. We deal with these kinds of situations all day long, every day. We *feel* them. Because life is a feeling and what you *feel* is real. Moreover, what you feel most frequently also becomes your reality.

While this may be tiresome, and yes, dukkha always is, these emotional moments are one of the greatest spiritual reasons we need a stronger, kinder society. Community offers you a huge benefit ignored by sociologists. Yes, it provides safety, companionship, and a tribal identity, but it also provides a mirror by which to study the state of your ego through the medium of your reactions to other people.

This may seem like some minor, almost *annoying* kind of reasoning, but it is actually another example of nature's brilliant construction. If we lived alone, we could do a good job of covering up who we are because we only have to deal with our own views, our own ideas, our own preferences, and our own desires, and so on. But in a group, there is no escaping the conflict of different people desiring a diverse set of objectives, and this gives us all frequent opportunities to feel our mighty ego awaken and react to situations in which it causes us to lose control.

Society is a powerful melting pot of subtle and not-so-subtle daily events that trigger your suffering. As you feel disappointment, joy, sadness, or jealousy, it is like your reality is staring back at you saying, "Here I am. This is real. Now, what will you do about it?" This is what is meant by dukkha. *This* is suffering. But I do not believe this is a reason to be miserable at all. Quite the opposite, in fact. Life is your science project and society is your microscope. This is your chance to ask that one incredible question: "Why do I feel like this?" The answer, in short, is not that nature is just messing with you. It is the laws of nature, coaxing you to be kinder to yourself.

Life is a wonder, and your life experiences are a heady mix of the glorious, painful, happy, exciting, and depressing. It doesn't matter that life is an emotional roller-coaster ride. What matters is learning how to love the dipping soaring turns of every beautiful maneuver that shapes it. Indeed, in a perfect partnership, society and nature work seamlessly to demonstrate why we suffer and how we can relieve ourselves of the burden.

Life's idiosyncrasies may toss you under the bus one day or heave you up to the heights of the tallest oak the next. You may often feel like a passenger on the train, not the driver, but the question is not really whether you *have* control of the external events, but whether you *take* control of the internal reaction. How do you handle the sensations in your mind and body, both the highs and the lows, that spring up as events transpire moment by moment? What do you do with the emotional blips triggered when life's tragedy whizzes by the windows of your carriage? As the 'Ooohs' and 'Aaahs' of your personal journey through wonderland ring long and loud in your ears, how do you handle the tide of sensations that will determine whether you enjoy the ride or hate every second of it?

The truth is that nature is teaching you how to deal with your emotions, and society is the perfect medium by which to evoke them. But in the twenty-first century, these two crucial pillars of human evolution have clashed. They are at odds with one another. Competition, independence, and selfish material objectives have twisted the social learning platform so that nature's interdependence can no longer breach the thick wall of consumerism that wrests our attention away from the inner world in which we create the outer world. Society ceases to offer us a way out of dukkha and it certainly doesn't admit it exists in the way that it does exist. In fact, it does the very opposite, which is where the problems begin to deepen. CLD trains us to ignore most of the shit that happens, handle only the shit we can't ignore, and cover up the rest of the shit with pizza, beer, and sex.

Or maybe that's just me. And if it is just me, a mental note, Mike: that *doesn't* work. It *has never* worked. It *will* never work. Oops! There goes, not only 13,000 years of so-called civilization. But also 51 years of my ill-placed faith in Domino's!

Chapter 4

Evolution of Mind

Overcome suffering? What are you talking about? Isn't that impossible?

In the previous chapter, Buddhadasa makes a powerful claim: "We must *collectively* attempt to *overcome* our common problem, dukkha...(through this) *God can be known.*" On superficial reflection, this claim seems to be nothing less than outrageous hyperbole. No one believes that emotional pain, physical trauma, or mental anguish can be *overcome*, do they? It's not like taking a Matrix pill that ends one reality and begins the next!

And no one is saying it is. Change takes time, but the problem we face today is that conventional wisdom has gripped our minds, and it isn't very wise. It doesn't tackle the root causes of suffering at all. On the contrary, the smartest minds in the world are gaining kudos from stimulating those root causes to grow the global economy around an illusion. We're not being taught to end suffering but to deepen it, to exacerbate the problem.

When you realize the causes of dukkha, Buddhadasa's deliberate use of the word 'overcome' makes more sense. It suggests not only that there is a way to *transcend* suffering completely but also that society has a key role in preparing each of us to master the method for ourselves. Wow! Imagine that! A society in which people are taught to end their suffering; the ultimate society; the ultimate compassion for all people; a way to teach everyone how to let go of dukkha: We-Topia. But rational people do not consider such a world a realistic prospect because our idea of progress has become so distorted. And, sadly, one of the key ingredients of this distortion is our very warped idea of what evolution even means.

When Darwin published *On the Origin of Species* in 1859, he spoke only of the physical processes by which nature evolves the multitude of organic life forms in the world. This is why popular culture still summarizes his findings as 'survival of the fittest' and often contextualizes that in terms of *competitive* prowess. This misconception underpins much of the machismo that supports a culture of social competition to determine winners and losers. Competitive society is natural selection in action, so we're told, and the fittest of us all will naturally rise to the surface to form the ranks of our most trustworthy leadership.

But what the public is not told is that, for the benefit of *this* competition, the losers will be armed with stones while the winner will drive tanks!

Another factor is that Darwin did not address the question of mental evolution, but it should not be a great leap of faith for us to see that physical and mental evolution happens in concert, one with the other. Just as the human body has evolved from apes into *Homo erectus* and now *Homo sapiens*, it is scientifically proven that the very architecture of the brain can change too:

One example of this is the well-known London cab driver studies which showed that the longer someone had been driving a taxi, the larger their hippocampus, a part of the brain involved in visual-spatial memory. Their brains literally expanded to accommodate the cognitive demands of navigating London's tangle of streets.[1]

As the brain learns, its architecture transforms. Indeed, learning even affects our DNA. The University of Georgia social psychologist, Dr. Abraham Tesser, notes: "the idea that a behavioral system has a strong genetic component is hardly an issue anymore." The component that links body and behavior together is *the mind*. But sometimes, popular culture can take a while to catch up. In this case, it's taken thousands of years, possibly tens of thousands, for modern people to begin to realize what their ancestors knew: the most rapid and profound form of evolution is possible in the area of the mind. Moreover, this is a process that doesn't take a million years, a thousand years, or even a few hundred. It is a phenomenon that you, and only you, can begin and see through to its conclusion in the course of *one lifetime*. It is literally what you were born to do!

Anecdotal evidence of this has existed for millennia and I will share even more of it in Chapter 12 when we discuss the idea of intelligence from a broader perspective of how the mind attains evolution. But for now, we can see that history is rife with stories of masters, teachers, gurus, and prophets, all attesting to the same thing: within every human being is a vast sea of spiritual potential that is accessed through the doors of the mind.

The life of Buddha attests to this. Not only did he achieve complete liberation from suffering, but his very first teaching was also the Four Noble Truths. This succinctly explains how suffering arises, why it recurs, and how to overcome it using natural philosophy and practice. Indeed, a great way of looking at the entire philosophical premise of Buddhism is as a 2500-year-old wellness guide to unlocking the secret phenomenon of liberty for all.

Here's the thing to remember: nobody claims that Buddha was superhuman. Least of all himself! He was as human as you or me. He had doubts, fears, anger, frustration, and everything else that you and I feel every day. His life has been memorialized because it demonstrated to us all that suffering is a choice[2] and we can free the mind from it through several basic practices that include mindfulness and a little study of natural reality. I understand that many people are turned off from spiritual study because religion is not their cup of tea, but the beauty of Buddha's teachings is that they were neither superstitious nor irrational. He directly addressed the problem of suffering in a scientific way that any one of us can grasp, practice, and see if it makes sense in our life.

Most poignantly, Buddha's life delivers a powerful lesson to us all: "Being born as a human is enough to end suffering forever." He achieved it. And so can you. This demonstrates that the method is universal, practical, and attainable, regardless of who you are, where you were born, or your cultural identity. Indeed, the tenets of this philosophy are so universal, it is instantly apparent that they can form the foundation of an effective social system anywhere and for anyone.

For example, the Buddha founded the *sangha*, the community of Buddhist monks, 2500 years ago, but today it is still going strong. It is a living illustration of how a strong social culture can endure through history. Again, this demonstrates that the concepts underpinning the idea of suffering and how to overcome it are not pie-in-the-sky thinking at all. To have survived for two and a half millennia, these ideas must be practical, attainable, and help people in meaningful ways.

Ironically, the fact that the sangha is a religious society has led to one of the most frequent criticisms of Dhamma; that it may work in a strict ascetic community, but it is not *practical* enough to be applied to a more general social system. But when we assess that argument logically, it is full of holes.

If the statistics that defined CLD in our last chapter were anything to go by, we would have to stretch our imaginations a mighty distance to call its systems *practical*. Ask yourself, which is more practical: learning a way to deal with the reality that has resulted in a peaceful society of people for two and a half thousand years? Or building a society that, in just fifty years, has conditioned the human mind to accept an unnatural state as its reality, while creating dissatisfaction, inequality, mental sickness, and ecological destruction in its wake?

I know which of those sounds *practical* to me. And while a society focused on eliminating suffering may seem a stretch on first appraisal, it is all just a matter of perspective. We should not and must not equate impractical with difficult or inconvenient. Change is never the easiest option: inertia is. But the time has come to realize that humanity is failing to live up to its potential. We are stuck. We are atrophying. And to save the patient, we have to take some strong medicine.

Look at the medicine like this: you, me, and everyone else in the world have been conditioned to perceive the existing power structures of the world as essential and irreplaceable. Just like we heard in 2008, CLD is too big to fail! If *you* were monopolizing the power, that's exactly what you'd want everyone else to think, wouldn't you? But when you compare the madness of the current world against the prospect of a society purposed towards spiritual evolution, what do you find? Surely a natural society focused on eliminating suffering is no less ridiculous than an unnatural society that manufactures bottle tops, Styrofoam, and cushion filler in order that you can afford shelter and buy food! Indeed, if you were born into a society today that taught you to demand the right to pursue your evolution, wellbeing, peace, and meaning, and not just own a new iPhone, that would seem perfectly normal to you too.

To remain relevant, CLD *requires* behaviors from you that no truly social system should ever demand. It requires your labor for the greater benefit of someone other than yourself. It requires your debt. It requires you to remain ignorant of why you are suffering and how you can end it. It requires a hierarchy in which a few people will be more powerful than the rest put together. This is not hyperbole. The systems of banking, corporations, and consumerism couldn't exist without those attitudes remaining reasonable enough to stop us from going ape about how ridiculous it all is! This hierarchy of unnatural values can only function effectively if you consent to be a consumer and chase your satisfaction through materials. Without these requirements being met by you and me, CLD would cease to exist. Yet, most citizens find these obligations perfectly *acceptable*, perfectly *normal*, and hardly an inconvenience.

Ladies and gentlemen, this is not any kind of reality. It is manufactured consent. It is a corrupted approval. It is a perversion of life's clear purpose: *overcoming suffering*. This purpose is not a nice-to-have objective. It is no fanciful dream of the spiritually zealous. It is your birthright. The evolution of your mind is nature's gift to you as it is to us all. In contrast, to seek evolution in a social system that requires your suffering to persist is madness. It is cruel. It is shameful. It is nigh on *impossible*.

The stunning truth is that we can choose to build a society that is not focused on wealth, consumerism, or materialism. We *can* select a society that is focused on our evolution. That is a *real* community of humankind. Moreover, unlike the fantasy of a society that tells you we can forever consume more and more and, one day, if we all work hard enough, we will all be wealthy, the reality of interdependence is no destructive myth! It is We-Topia: a society that aspires to the highest principles of humanity, reflecting the highest values of nature.

Agreed, the road to such a society is a long one, but at least it starts with truth. It has no pretense; nor does it seek to obscure reality from you under the pretext of liberty, equality, or fraternity. Indeed, We-Topia is an idea that is truly free because its objective is freedom from dukkha, nature's ultimate message to us all. And that freedom isn't for me, or them or someone else; it's for *you*. It's up to you whether you choose that kind of freedom. But to make that choice without bias, without hindrance, and without prejudice, we must all understand that we have all been lied to for a long time.

A very, very, *very* long time.

Chapter 5

Our Spiritual Heritage

Buddhadasa stated in *Dhammic Socialism*: "The goal of every religion is to put an end to self-centeredness, to a 'me' and 'mine' kind of thinking."[1] This mentality stems from the mind, the *ego*, and can be observed at work in today's obsession with personal identity and image. One needs to look no further than the explosion of social media sites to see this mental phenomenon flourishing.

The antidote to this way of thinking is not hard to find, but few of us notice when we see or hear it. It plays quietly in the interdependence of nature and in the background noise of one's own mind. In nomadic times, this spiritual melody would have been a constant soundtrack to our lives. After all, what else was there to focus on in a forest or beside a lake? As nomads, freely roaming the planet, we couldn't fail but feel "the calming effects of the natural environment," as Buddhadasa put it. We would have experienced the "'socialist' thoughts and feelings (that) arise from such a calm state." We would have known that the world is but "earth, water, air, fire, and consciousness." And most significantly, there would have been "no deceit, no 'me/mine' distinctions." They simply would not exist because the ultimate lesson of no-self would have been glaringly obvious to us.

This intimate relationship between humanity and nature sits at the root of everything we call *spiritual*. Sadly, spirituality gets a bad rap because it is so often misrepresented by false ideas and insincere ambitions. Plus, it's big business. However, to simplify the meaning of the word 'spiritual' in *We-Topia*, let me define it as the deeper connection of your body, mind, and energy to the laws of nature: to Dhamma.

When we investigate the legacy of human spiritual belief, we find that Dhamma was always the purpose of spirituality: to heighten the connection of humankind to our roots in the laws of nature. Spirituality is not supposed to turn us into fluffy hopers and dreamers. It is supposed to guide us to *think* more, *do* more, and *live* more aligned with the reality of nature, rather than the selfish aspirations of the human ego.

Sadly, in modern times, religion and spirituality have become conflated despite having starkly different purposes. The essence of spirituality is freedom from artificial control and order. It hankers for the chaos and unpredictability of the natural world, unconstrained by the demands of ego to limit and control. But the same cannot be said for religion. Indeed, religion *is* the control system, molding raw spiritual passion into an ordered and homogenized structure of social constraints.

To understand when and why spirituality became religion we have to look back and identify the prevailing motivations of humanity as we transitioned from hunter-gathers in a nomadic society to sedentary farmers in agricultural communities.

Imagine the world 20,000 years ago. Imagine the slow pervasive effect of permanently living out under the sun, the stars, in the elements of this world, ensconced in the seasons, the weather, the process of life and death, and every natural pattern in between. You would be entrained with nature. You would have surrendered to nature like it was your very own God. Add to this an egalitarian social structure unimpeded by controls and unhindered by limits, and we would then have no need to rein in our imaginations or to insulate ourselves from illusory threats. In this world, in this mind, one is naturally drawn to explore the unity of life, the vastness of space, and the interdependence of nature, not because you are an unsophisticated prehistoric cave-dweller, but because of human curiosity. It is there, right before your eyes! It is your reality. And you want to know how it works.

However, this curiosity isn't conventionally scientific. It is a personal, internal exploration that shapes every single person in the entire community. Undisturbed by technology and thoroughly immersed in the laws of nature, we become supremely conscious of the thoughts, feelings, reactions, responses, and emotions that take root in our minds. To us, nature was the ultimate reality TV: *reality!* With "no deceit, no 'me/mine' distinctions" to distract us, our brilliant minds were less clouded, clearer, more agile. Rather than spending hours in front of a shiny screen, nomads explored the vagaries of their minds, not motivated by the final boss of a video game but exploring the complexities of their own ego, the biggest final boss of them all.

Their game room would have been the Earth, nature's arcade reverberant with a multitude of tastes, sounds, smells, colors, and feelings that we hold on to as *I, me,* and *mine.* They didn't need self-help gurus or personal development programs to guide them. The stark simplicity of the environment was enough to coax observation of their emotions ebbing and flowing like the tides, rising and falling like the sun.

Through the fears of the forest and the abundance of the grove, life's impermanence was showcased in vivid splendor, encouraging us to stitch together a great philosophy of letting go, of non-attachment, of selfless awakening that managed suffering in an unforgiving world. In short, the natural systems of the Earth grounded the mind in spiritual truth, funneling experience towards mental evolution. In such a world, spiritual evolution would have been routine, commonplace, and swift. And there would have been no shortage of volunteers for the journey.

The prehistoric world had no organized systems of worship. Each tribe had its own collection of practices, ideas, poems, stories, and analogies that addressed the problem of dukkha and ego by shaping minds, values, and ethics. We passed this understanding down through the generations in songs, mythologies, and legends that evoked a higher morality because our ancestors were gravely aware of the threat posed by the ego. They understood very well that it not only threatened our grounding in the natural reality but also presented a real and present danger to the tribe's unity and power. If the ego were allowed to compete and dominate, it would mean the end of us all.

With no means of writing down their beliefs, prehistoric spiritual traditions were orally transmitted. In ancient tribes across this world, wise family members taught their kids the Great Truths of the Tribe like they were sharing flakes of spiritual gold dust. They made these profound lessons into stories, into poems, into the tales of gods and heroes and morality stories that taught, not the absolute scientific truth of nature, but *the way to shape good human nature*. That was not only the perfect survival tool we all needed, but also a more profound truth than Newton's Laws could ever be. And those rules were told so often that the children were required to remember the teachings word for word. The minds of these students became the time capsules for this profound resource, for they were the future teachers who would pass on the traditions to the next generation so that they in turn could pass on the traditions in the same way.

How long could such oral traditions survive? Thousands and thousands of years! A great example is the Hindu Veda, a tradition so strict, it is best left to an encyclopedia to describe its feats:

The Vedas existed in oral form and were passed down from master to student for generations until they were committed to writing between c. 1500—c. 500 BCE (the so-called Vedic Period) in India. They were carefully preserved orally as masters would have students memorize them forwards and backwards with emphasis on exact pronunciation in order to keep what was originally heard intact.[2]

Forwards and backwards? Wow! And to think that I used to moan at my teachers about learning a few multiplication tables by rote! Imagine learning thousands of lines of information, both forwards and backwards, as your homework!

Another example of this oral tradition is the Torah, written down in the first century CE (Common Era) but, prior to this, believed by scholars to have been handed down orally for at least 1500 years. These traditions of unbroken testimony are vast, but they merely hint at the potential of the human mind. Tribal elders in Aboriginal Australia have recalled an account of a volcanic eruption for around *35,000 years!* Evidence suggests that entire philosophies could have survived intact for tens of millennia, passed on using the kinds of mnemonic recall that we marvel at today. All they needed was the right kind of motivation. And what greater motivation would we need than *to protect the very spiritual evolution of our species from the threat of ego?*

But today, much of this tradition has been misunderstood. The Old Testament story of Adam and Eve is a perfect example, pulling no punches in its description of what would happen if humanity ate the fruit from the Tree of Knowledge: "then your eyes shall be opened, and ye shall be as gods, knowing good and evil."[3] At its most fundamental level, this is a description of what happens when the ego becomes a greater arbiter of truth than nature itself. Is there a more suitable metaphor for today, living in a world where applications of science define our moral compass and values?

In the Vedas, much like in the Abrahamic texts, there is a focus on the effects of ego, namely the sins. While the Old Testament speaks of Seven Cardinal Sins, the Veda focuses on lust and anger, two key ways in which the ego impresses itself onto the world through physical and emotional desire. It also speaks of creation as being a process of devolving divine energy into the material form, rather like the notion of Adam and Eve 'falling' from paradise into the mundane world of 'the knowledge of good and evil.'

Zoroastrianism, a Middle Eastern religion believed to have begun around the second millennium BCE (Before the Common Era), prescribed a threefold path consisting of good thoughts, good words, and good deeds. Through this formula of living, one could embrace Asha, truth and cosmic order, and reject Druj, which is falsehood and deceit. These are yet more synonyms for what we would call ego today.

Across the modern world, we find ancient spiritual concepts embedded deeply into religions. Relatively recent prophets such as Christ, Muhammad, and Buddha founded their ideas on these ancient precursor philosophies because the ideas in them were timeless. These masters were not the founders of entirely *new* ideas. They resuscitated ancient concepts, reinvigorated them with new techniques, and delivered them in ways appropriate for their contemporary audience.

People often distrust spirituality because of its negative affiliation with religion. This is both sad and ironic. The spiritual precursors taught ideas and skills that most modern people are denied today through their strict diet of materialism. Modern religion repackaged ascetic ideas into spiritual materialism, a system of idolatry, rewards, salvation, and exclusivity that spiritual traditions specifically warned us against creating! Remember the Tower of Babel, for example? Yeah, that. And Islam has no images of Muhammad for a good reason: a warning against the trappings of idolatry and selfhood.

The examples are innumerable, but the irony goes even deeper. Prehistoric spiritual traditions would not only balk at the religions they have been co-opted into, but were their ideas taught to the world today, they would be considered nothing short of *subversive*. They would challenge and contradict the integrity of every social structure erected to suppress those ideas. This message, communicated by all the precursor spiritual traditions, can be summed up in one biblical text: 'behold, the kingdom of God is within you."[4]

What's so subversive about that? Well, imagine you lived eight or nine thousand years ago and try to place yourself in the minds of the many emperors, kings, and would-be tyrants of the time. How would you feel about a popular and influential belief system claiming that each individual was a personal source of God-like power? It undermined the credibility of your rule, didn't it? How do you maintain citizens of malleable minds consenting to your domination if you allow the population to evolve a spiritually mature belief in the absolute supremacy of their personal power?

Ancient spirituality reflected everything natural and real about the world. It didn't embrace artificial power structures; it questioned them. It didn't cede to earthly authority, but a higher truth. And it didn't need intermediaries to build a relationship with God. He was everywhere and in everything. You could meet Him yourself. Just look at a flower, chase a rabbit, watch the stars, feel the rain: be alive! And there He was, right inside you, the ultimate power of creation at your fingertips!

No, no, *no!* This would never do. The top echelon of the social pyramid needed to manufacture an unwavering belief in the population that the ultimate authority on this Earth was earthly knowledge, the intelligentsia, and the self-appointed elite. If the hoi polloi realized they were blessed with the power to free themselves, on what grounds could their subjugation to rulers be justified?

What ensued was the mightiest power struggle the world has ever known: *systems of the ego versus systems of the spirit*. It was a power struggle to determine *which* truth would win the philosophical war and shape the future cultures of the Earth. And, 13,000 years later, the battle has been won. The victor is the truth of ego. And its system of control is called Capitalist Liberal Democracy.

Chapter 6

From Free Spirituality to Organized Religion

Thirteen thousand years ago, the Neolithic Revolution sounded the death knell for personal spiritual traditions. It was the beginning of a long, slow decline in human spiritual evolution characterized by a gradual shift into an increasingly polarized and structured social hierarchy.

Before this, historical research shows that egalitarianism was relatively common in nomadic tribes. Indeed, the author and historian, Karen Endicott, studied African tribes today and found that most are egalitarian and practice gender equality.[1] However, sedentary village life encouraged a very different kind of social structure. It augured skill specialization and a pecking order in society to the point where, over time, farmers became village chiefs, village chiefs became kings, and kings became emperors. Around these new fixed communities, legal, military, political, and commercial structures grew, each supporting a stratified society that began to tell people something they had never heard before: we are not equal. From the nomad to the farmer and the farmer to the factory worker and the factory worker to the office worker, over thousands of years, the world gradually became more and more like we know it today: unequal.

During this long transition and slow stratification, there was a problem. Spiritual traditions stood in the way of this so-called progress. To organize a structured society, you need roles and authority with leaders and followers. In an egalitarian society, that can be done through situational leadership, but it's easy to misinterpret the idea if you create fixed positions with permanent authority. At this point, people are no longer equal. Society is forever changed.

The problem was, for thousands of years before this movement into sedentary communities, spiritual traditions had insisted that every person on this Earth was born equal, each individual was as powerful as the next, and everyone had the same potential to transcend the bonds of suffering. We know this because that is what the great precursor religions were all saying. However, it seems that the great alpha personalities of this world had other ideas. They saw that progress was a matter of pushing through change and, if needed, taking control of the tribe to do so. What use was a spiritual vision of egalitarianism to them in a community with an emerging power structure in which they saw the opportunity to dominate?

As more tribes settled and villages flourished, material possessions grew too. This presented a unique temptation to connect positional authority to social value and social value to the sum of possessions you deserved to keep for yourself. However, still standing in the way of this beautifully selfish idea was a spiritual teaching that exists to this day, that the mass accumulation of personal property is a character flaw. Some call it greed, others avarice; still more term it covetousness; but whatever it is called, all spiritual traditions warn against the ego's tendency to desire property that artificially inflates its sense of selfhood. What our village antagonists needed was a way to repress this annoying little idea, assert subtle control over these spiritual teachings, and begin accumulating wealth, power, and influence for their own grandeur.

In *Provolution*, I quoted the inimitable Jiddu Krishnamurti, a quote well worth repeating here. In 1911, he disbanded the Order of the Star, a religion with 3000 members who had been awaiting his birth and ascendancy. He did so by telling them the following joke:

You may remember the story of how the devil and a friend of his were walking down the street, when they saw ahead of them a man stoop down and pick up something from the ground, look at it, and put it away in his pocket.

The friend said to the devil, "What did that man pick up?"

"He picked up a piece of Truth," said the devil.

"That is a very bad business for you, then," said his friend.

"Oh, not at all," the devil replied, "I am going to let him organize it."

To Krishnamurti, this story was no mere quip. He knew the ease with which useful spiritual traditions could be co-opted into methods of mass control. If the chaotic, personal nature of these traditional practices was centralized, structured, depersonalized, and projected as a vehicle for conformity, its message could be corrupted and its power to suppress egotistic megalomania would be quashed. Rather than being a counterweight to the rise of this new social order, organized spirituality could become a powerful proponent of it.

Indeed, the totality of this compliance is self-evident in today's society. In the last 2500 years, the world has been carved up into 16 major religious denominations[2] and hundreds of subsects within those categories. Roughly 84% of the global population now associates their faith with one of these organized structures.[3] Like the societies from which they emerged, they have become globalized, each embracing organizational apparatus whose roots have burrowed so deeply into our social paradigms that some have even been integrated into the political apparatus of nation-states.

Even in countries that are supposed to be secular, religious ideology bleeds over into politics, influencing key moral issues from birth control to capital punishment and sexuality to race relations. The authentic heart of our traditional natural beliefs beats no more, its spirit of unity through no-self supplanted in the legislatures of the world by politicians who sing artificial melodies of love, compassion, and hope from the cockpits of their bombers and the boardrooms of the banks. These voices do not want a fairer world. They have no notion of equality or how to create it. They will not struggle for the fairness they pretend to envision in their public speeches and proclamations. In the closet of their own mind, they want the world to remain exactly the way it is, a place where they have the power and control, a place where they win.

Besides, how could any truly authentic voice today stand up against these enduring institutions that have stood the test of time? As entire civilizations have been born and died away, religions have straddled the millennia like Titans. Political institutions are mere paper tigers in comparison to the religions that entreat billions to believe in their promise of spiritual freedom. But their greatest power is not the kernel of spiritual emancipation that dangles from their doctrine but the way in which they have organized obedience in our populations and convinced the entire world that we need a middleman to be free.

Indeed, most religions today advocate on behalf of spiritual evolution about as credibly as M&Ms advocate nutrition. It would be disingenuous to suggest that M&Ms are a health product simply because they have a high-potassium peanut at their core. In the same way, it's not credible to claim that religion is truly invested in your spiritual freedom because it mentions love and charity. To believe this about M&Ms, you'd have to ignore a rather prominent layer of chocolate. To believe it about most religions, you would have to ignore their banks, their hoards of priceless artworks, their history of covering up sexual violence, their history of advocating non-sexual violence, an estimated financial worth of $30 billion,[4] oh, and their stores of gold and precious metals to the sum of $50 million that they keep for a rainy day.[5]

That's just a random example, by the way. (*cough*)

Buddhadasa knew this process of religious deterioration all too well when he said:

All religions begin as a kind of applied science, but gradually they tend to become more a matter of mere words or logic or philosophy, moving further and further from actual practice.[6]

And *that* was precisely the greatest and most insidious achievement of ego's victory over spirit. By managing spiritual ideas, by building hierarchy, by manipulating the power structures and by insisting upon priestly middlemen, we were distanced from our own personal divine potential. We took a step back from being in touching distance of unfettered freedom and supplanted our deeply personal practice with ritual, rite, and ceremony centralized and ordered by an external authority.

There is a very simple test to determine if any religion is what it says it is: ask *why* it exists. If it is truly interested in your spiritual liberty then, not surprisingly, *you* will be the purpose of its existence. It will be humble. It will be poor. It would give everything to you so that you might see the divinity of your own no-self. The very purpose of its existence would be to free you from the grip of the material world, to unleash your potential and leave nothing between you and your destiny.

Yet, is that what religion does? Do we ignore the wealth, pomp, and ceremony of religions as part and parcel of the grandeur it needs to project authority or does all of that excess simply make my point for me? Sadly, little humility can be found in modern religious organizations. They rarely advocate freedom and self-exploration but have become the mouthpiece of pre-existing social value structures (hierarchy, rules, blame, punishment, and so on). While they seemingly temper the worst excesses of those systems (such as hate, greed, fear) and champion values we can embrace as divine (charity, love, kindness), they actually change nothing fundamental about the way we have been taught to think and behave (exclusively, competitively, and in absolutes). This is Krishnamurti's greatest fear realized—organization of the unorganizable into the unusable. They are Trojan horses that do just enough for us to believe they are helpful, but not enough to change the status quo they are meant to dismantle.

History tolls long and loud with a warning of how the greatest spiritual truth ever told became just another pillar in the accumulation of ego's power on the Earth. Today, religions sit snugly within the value system of CLD, espousing a kind of spiritual materialism whose ideas are eerily similar. They both claim that their religion/economic system is the only one that knows God/social progress. They both insist that their priests/scientists are infallible. And, while appearing outwardly inclusive and tolerant, both insist that other religions/social systems are sinful/morally corrupt, and will send you straight to hell/economic ruin.

CLD didn't corrupt religion any more than religion corrupted CLD. They are both manifestations of an attitude that evolved over thousands of years. The comedian Ricky Gervais said: "Spirituality really lost its way when it became a stick to beat people with: 'Do this or you'll burn in hell.'" Very true, but losing its way wasn't the fault of spirituality any more than we could say that science lost its way when engineers built the atomic bomb.

What CLD and religion both reflect is our busted moral compass. But what is less obvious is that those people who forged a winning position from its destruction deliberately busted our moral compass. The truth is that *anything* exclusively organized by ego will be corrupted because ego, in this form, is *the corruption*. It is the antithesis of spirit, which was formerly invigorated by ancient teachings continually refreshed over the millennia. Today, many of these teachings are corrupted, but that doesn't mean they don't exist. Co-opting esoteric teachings to manufacture consent from the populace is not the fault of spirituality; it is an inevitable result of the ego-genie being uncorked from its bottle.

The gradual historical *accumulation* of ego in society is evident for all to see. Our world is now embroiled in so much religious scandal[7] that the words of Jiddu Krishnamurti could not ring louder, stronger, or more profoundly were they sung in chorus from the roof of Saint Peter's, the shrine of the Kaaba, the stupa of Bodh Gaya, or the Temple Mount of Jerusalem itself. In *Dhammic Socialism* Buddhadasa made a powerful statement:

If we drive a car off the road and halfway into a ditch, what can we do? We must back up and get back onto the road so that we can go on driving. This is the situation of the human race these days. We have left the correct way, the way of Dhamma, the way of God, or whatever one may call it. We have strayed far from that way, quite far, indeed—so far that one might say we have turned our backs on religion, on God, on the Dhamma. If we push on like this much further, we will fall into the abyss.[8]

While this chapter has been a warning about the existing systems in which we have misplaced our faith, for thousands of years the ego had already been identified as the culprit of all conflict, greed, and hatred in the world. We *knew* that it was the cause of all suffering. We recognized that it eroded the community. And we also understood that ego was a *creation*, a choice, a conditioned manifestation that we could either embrace and live with while suffering, or *liberate ourselves from and live in peace.*

But, even then, despite knowing all of this, we still drove off the road and into the ditch.

Chapter 7

The Three Marks of Existence

We have identified CLD as a social system causing needless suffering in the world. We have learned how overcoming this suffering is the clear purpose of life and all spiritual practice that is worthy of the name. And we have read how Buddhadasa believed the most practical spiritual practice was to "overcome our common problem, *dukkha*, by doing whatever will bring us to a fuller understanding of the term *Dhamma*." So, having looked at the roots of dukkha, the only question we now face is the obvious next step: what is Dhamma and what does it teach us about subduing suffering?

In the next two chapters, we are going to review two crucial aspects of Buddha's teachings, known as Buddha-Dhamma. In this chapter, we will look at three facets of natural reality and, in the following chapter, we will investigate how suffering is created in the mind. The purpose of this detour is to furnish the reader with a deeper insight into the basic dynamics of the internal/external world, mind and nature, all of which society has ignored. This is the crux of all social problems. By digging a little deeper into this spiritual philosophy, we will see how crucial this knowledge is in redressing society's imbalance and offering us all an opportunity to pursue life's deeper meaning for ourselves.

Let's start with simply understanding the word 'Dhamma.' While it has no direct translation into English, Buddhadasa always simplified its meaning as 'the laws of nature' and equated these laws with God. He said:

Religion belongs to the realm of science in that it combines both theory and application. All religions address basic human problems with empirical methods derived from observing cause and effect.[1]

This implies three key things. Firstly, that Buddha-Dhamma, the laws of nature, is no more an invention of Buddha than gravity was an invention of Newton. Secondly, that you, me, or anyone else can observe the basic causes of our human problems as they arise. And thirdly that, if we can observe the causes of these problems, it is also within our power to end them.

The word 'Dhamma' was common in Vedic philosophy for millennia before Buddha was born. What sets Buddha's Dhamma apart is that he went deeper and further than any other practitioner before him. Note, I say *practitioner*, not teacher, prophet, guru, philosopher, or any of these other words that imply a person who possesses and communicates knowledge. Buddha, first and foremost, was a doer. He attained his insight by experiencing suffering in his life, diligently observing the causes of it in his mind, and then, through hard work, penetrating to solutions that removed those causes altogether. What makes his extraordinary achievement unique is that his teachings were a practice, *a way of life*. There is no faith involved. If you or I understand his ideas and practice them, we too will experience the freedom from suffering that Buddha experienced.

Of course, pure Buddha-Dhamma has many aspects to it that are unnecessary for us to cover here. Indeed, my intention is not to promote Buddhism in any shape or form (I cannot claim to be a Buddhist myself) but to simply convey the idea that life's purpose is known and, thousands of years ago, a secular strategy was developed to achieve it. Just a few key lessons from Buddha's teachings are enough to exemplify that there is a practical fact-based method of attaining a better, more practical society. This is not a sectarian or religious path. It is about integrating natural processes into our minds and observing if they are more effective than the results we are currently getting with CLD.

The first concept I would like to introduce is called the Three Marks of Existence, a set of three very simple ideas that define reality for what it is and correct some basic misconceptions about life. Its core ideas are *impermanence, unsatisfactoriness,* and *no-self.* Let's cover each of these now, one by one, so that we can use these three beautiful little ideas as a foundation for the rest of the book.

1. Impermanence

Impermanence is the concept that everything in nature is in a state of perpetual motion and change. This might seem self-evident, but you'd be surprised how often we all ignore it completely! Buddha's dying words were: "All conditioned things are impermanent. Work diligently." So, if Buddha considered impermanence important enough to refer to with his dying breath, we should certainly consider it important enough to wonder: "Why?"

If I had to summarize what Buddha's teachings meant to me I'd say this: Buddha taught people to destroy mental illusions and see the world for how it is, not how we think, believe, or hope it is. The greatest problem in the world today is viewing the world through the fog of assumptions, misconceptions, and illusions. We *all* do it. The only variable is how deeply we subscribe to the illusions. While we live in an age of science, facts, and data, the irony is that people are less able than ever to 'see things as they are.' What we can deduce from this is that having more information at our fingertips has not made people *wiser.* It has only rendered us *more certain that our misconceptions are the truth.*

Failing to truly respect the impermanence of the world is a profound example of failing to see things as they are. While impermanence exists in all things and at all times, your mind clings to the identity of those things as permanent, often assuming, misconstruing, or simply hoping that they remain stable and constant. This belief causes suffering that takes three basic forms:

- **Physical:** e.g., you're *afraid* your spanking new phone might get damaged.
- **Emotional:** e.g., you're *shocked* by your child's new haircut and nose ring.
- **Mental:** e.g., people who disagree with your opinion usually *frustrate* you.

Each of these emotional reactions seems very normal, given the examples above, but they are all caused by a mental desire to *maintain* something in its present state. That's the opposite of accepting impermanence. Think about how often we do that. We want our phones to remain new, our children to remain within the limits of our expectations, and for others to agree with our opinions!

Moreover, you have *taught* your mind to believe that it is *possible* to maintain this impossible balance, or even that you have the right to do so, but it is an unnatural expectation, at best an illusion, and at worst a cause of long-term suffering! All of us found our quest for a happier life upon impermanent objects, situations, and people remaining fixed and stable. That's a foundation of quicksand in a naturally unstable and impermanent world. It's no wonder we are so frequently disappointed!

Doesn't it make sense to condition the mind to see everything as impermanent, rather than hoping, expecting, or dreaming that a situation, person, or object will remain unnaturally stable forever? Unfortunately, this is not what society teaches us, so it is not what any of us do. Rather, we pursue a policy of managing change by maintaining things in our heads in a form that appears familiar or comfortable to us. We try to *control* reality to be as we would like it to be, not how it is.

Effectively, this conforms the world to an illusion of the mind, rather than conforming our mind to the reality of the world. How helpful do you think that is? Whether it's an idea, belief, household item, memory, relationship, or living being, believing it is immutable doesn't make it so. It only creates conditions in your mind that conflict with nature, and the result is suffering: dukkha.

To effectively live with impermanence, you must first absorb its deepest meaning into your mind and then practice living it. This is what Buddha was referring to with his dying words, "Work diligently." He encouraged us, not just to *understand* the concept of impermanence, but also to *be it* in our minds and collectively manifest it in the society and culture in which we live and learn.

2. Unsatisfactoriness

Unsatisfactoriness sounds like a very depressing world to live in, but it's actually the opposite. When fully understood, perceiving the innate unsatisfactoriness of all experience *frees* us from chasing the very solutions to our unhappiness that cause it in the first place!

Here's how it works: think back through your experiences over the past 24 hours. Observe the impermanence of those events and, in particular, how yesterday's pleasant experiences came and went. Consider how you had to shift around on the sofa when a comfortable sitting position became painful, or the pleasantly warm sun became too hot to endure, or the lovely lunch you had gave you gas, or the joy of a big purchase left you worrying about credit card bills, or how your hair looked great in the morning but was a mess by the time you got home, or how you were feeling happy until a bad driver on the road caused you to become angry, or how you were playing a sport you loved but got frustrated by your losing streak, and so forth...

This is life, all day, every day. Happy moments become less happy, and less happy moments get better. When you deeply contemplate this pattern of experience, you will begin to realize that the human condition is a timeless and continuous flow of impermanent satisfaction and dissatisfaction. Whatever you do, wherever you go, whatever you own, whatever you achieve, you cannot sustain a feeling of satisfaction forever. It is not how reality is made.

While this may sound like a solely philosophical bummer, the fact is that science has identified this bummer too! Gödel's Incompleteness Theory warns that no theory can ever prove itself true. The implication is that, if you have a scientific theory, you will need a second theory to prove it, then a further theory to prove that one, and so on. The reality of the physical world presents us with an endless cycle of change that requires the perpetual input of energy to maintain a temporary state. It is like the heat in a cold winter cabin; unless we keep feeding the fireplace with more wood, the toasty temperature will drop, and suffering sets in. By the same token, the nature of your mind demands endless new pleasurable experiences to maintain that buzz of satisfaction. After one experience fades, it needs another, and another, and another, and another...

In short, unsatisfactoriness is not just a feeling. It is the way the universe is set up. So, it must have a reason for being there. What is its purpose? Is it to force us all to endlessly cut down and dig up nature to make temporary gadgets that amuse us for a while before we throw them away and buy new ones? Probably not.

Or is it to steel us against the illusion of constancy and control by adopting a more sustainable way to live in peace with impermanence? That sounds more like it.

The fact of the matter is that your joy is not determined by what you own or hold on to; it is determined by how you have trained your mind to accept what you have. Again, it is a bit weird that we can all intellectually accept the reality of impermanence and unsatisfactoriness but take no steps to train our minds so that society lives peacefully with it, isn't it? The beauty of Dhamma is that it not only prescribes a set of practices that tell us what the delusions are, but also reduces our reliance on chasing unsatisfactory experiences by practicing different things such as mindfulness, compassion, and surrendering to the moment.

Ultimately, more suffering arises in our minds, not just because unsatisfactoriness exists in the universe, but also because we mitigate it through foolish thoughts and behaviors. We all know that pleasant experiences are impermanent and unsatisfactory, so we try to avoid the low points by chasing the next thrill. There's nothing wrong with this approach. It's very natural. But if you maintain this strategy without knowing that it's a fine rendition of Gödel's Incompleteness Theory, you are condemning yourself to temporary solutions to life's most enduring problem.

This is a truly exhausting way to solve the problem of suffering: by *not* solving it. But our economy couldn't function if we all solved this problem forever, could it? Indeed, our inability to see things as they are is deepened by the way we have set society up. A good example is how marketeers manipulate our desires. It has become normal, commonplace, and acceptable for slick marketing campaigns to convince us that fulfilling our deepest desires is our best exit strategy from suffering. Their profits depend upon us believing this lie. Have a Coke! Go on holiday here! Drive that vehicle! Look like this, not like that! Buy a phone! Be a better person! Make a billion dollars! In the past, this mesmeric influence would have been called magic or sorcery. But today, it is a worthy profession. It is a perfect example of how acceptable it has become for our consumer culture to exploit human psychology. We sow seeds of delusion in our pursuit of wealth. Rather than actually addressing the universal issue of suffering common to all human beings, *society promotes suffering as a way of life and requires that you remain ignorant of its roots in order to maintain it!*

The monk, Ajarn Brahm, said in his book *Opening the Door of Your Heart*:

One can say that the underlying creed of most Western democracies is to protect their people's freedom to realise their desires, as far as this is possible. It is remarkable that in such countries people do not feel very free. The second kind of freedom, freedom from desires, is celebrated only in some religious communities. It celebrates contentment, peace that is free from desires.[2]

This statement is a stunning indictment of CLD. A society that fails to recognize the natural truth of unsatisfactoriness commits its citizens to endless suffering. So, why is it that only "some religious communities" practice freedom from desire? Must we all become monks and nuns and abstain from all forms of pleasure? No! Far from it! There is a middle path to this process available to anyone with an open mind.

3. No-self

No-self is an extremely subtle but powerful idea that ties impermanence and unsatisfactoriness together into the single most significant spiritual lesson you will ever learn. Yes, that's quite a claim, but as Buddhadasa himself said: "True happiness consists in eliminating the false idea of 'I'." This is the ultimate conclusion of realizing that nature is but a transient aggregate of interconnected parts. Everything rises and falls; it is born, grows, matures, and dies; nothing is stable or consistent, and within all this impermanence, there is no fundamental unit of 'me' or 'mine.'

Let's look deeper at what this means. In life, the physical body of every living creature is comprised of what it eats, drinks, and breathes. Consistent with scientific theory, elements form aggregates (for example, molecules or cells) that assume a temporary symbiotic state with one another until life ends. Then, the parts break down and aggregate into something else. This process is endless and perpetual. It never ever stops.

Furthermore, each scale of life is a container for all the ones below it. At the most infinitesimally small level are energy waves, made from bosons and quarks; then atomic elements are made from protons, electrons, and neutrons; next, molecules are made from atoms; then cells are comprised of molecules, and so on and so forth. It is like the Russian Matryoshka doll, one doll inside the next, scaling up until all you see is an identifiable 'body': a single physical form.

This is the way things are. But in this physical reality, there also exists the energy of mind, a highly subtle environment, far subtler than physical energy. It is in this ambiguous state that we each fashion an ego that thrives on...well...whatever it wants to believe. Primarily, these are illusions! Your ego is a vague image of yourself that is founded on very few facts at all. You visualize, talk about, and project yourself into the world day after day and all day long.

But the funny thing is, when I ask people in my workshops "Who are you?" many people struggle to answer. Indeed, most have never even pondered the question. When answers do eventually come, respondents generally claim to be a role (like a father, businessperson, woman, or teacher), an adjective (like good, compassionate, competitive, or kind), or a spiritual or religious trope (like a soul, energy, or a child of God), and so on. But this vague perception we have of ourselves is not only very misleading, the natural values of impermanence and unsatisfactoriness totally dispute its existence.

If a part of you were eternal, it would be fair to refer to that part or piece as being 'me' or 'mine.' But, in the real world, impermanence confirms that there is no constant 'self.' Everything can be broken down and has no eternal existence. For example, if you examine your body, you will identify nothing eternal there. Neither will you find any idea or belief in your mind that cannot change or be adjusted. Even the idea of a soul is energetic and therefore exists as an ever-changing energy form that has no immutable self within it. *You* are temporary, just like everything else.

You may argue, "Well, that's because '*I*' am the whole package, an aggregate of all my thoughts, feelings, and experiences," which is exactly my point. An aggregate of mind, body, and energy is, by its very nature, in constant flux. Who you think you are is an ever changing product of the moment in which you exist. There is no *me*. There is no *mine*. There is an ever-flowing creation, and that ever-flowing creation finds its most natural state when you stop trying to control its evolution by fixing it at times, places, events, and in an identity that you consider to be 'you' and 'yours.'

When you establish this concept in your mind, you will see that this reality of no-self exists in stark contrast to how you *actually* perceive yourself. In your world, you live in *your* body, which feels *your* feelings and contains *your* brain, in which you hold *your* values, based upon *your* truth, which has developed *your* characteristics, and you are in control of all that. And to an extent, it is true. You are independent of other people, and you do control some things, but in many ways, even this is impermanent.

In truth, you rely upon a temporary body, with temporary feelings, with a temporary knowledge made of flexible values, with an ever-changing truth that has built a character that is not who you are, yet feels like you, but is just an illusion of your choices stitched together. You do not possess any of those things as a permanent identity. You have merely *become* them: *temporarily*. It might be more accurate to suggest that many of these temporary conditions have become you. Your true identity, *no-self*, is hidden like a huge diamond buried in the center of a vast mountain of coal that you pressured into existence around it.

Everyone's self-image can be demonstrated to be illusory. We are all made from opinions and ideas that have been handed down to us by our family, teachers, and cultural influences, sometimes over generations. From one perspective, it is entirely necessary, for it gives us our sense of inclusion, purpose, confidence, and character.

However, it is also responsible for endlessly chasing impossible solutions to our suffering that blights all our lives. Indeed, the ego sits at the very root of why humanity created CLD in the first place. The ego feeds CLD and CLD feeds the ego. They justify each other's existence and are as co-dependent as the members of a mutually abusive relationship.

No-self is not a concept. It is not a theory. It is as much a reality of physics as gravity or electromagnetism. And while the truth of nature is very, very simple, it's hard to change a mind whose very identity is so dependent upon an illusion persisting.

The good news is that no-self is not reality because I tell you it is, or even because prophets have attested to it as such. It becomes real only when you witness it yourself, every day, in the impermanence and unsatisfactoriness of your life's reality. And when you witness it yourself in this way, you can begin to live in a reality that sees it everywhere you look.

***

There exists today, and has existed for thousands of years, the means of explaining why social conflict, extremism, and competition find such fertile soil in the world. The means of overcoming those scourges are not a mystery now, nor have they *ever* been. Sadly, contemporary power structures appear necessary to bring order to our lives and, by accepting that order, we overlook the inequity they support and the illusion of selfhood that rationalizes it into existence. The truth of the matter is that the structures of modern society not only exacerbate conflict, extremism, and competition where far less could or should be, they only do so because they fundamentally ignore the reality of the Three Marks of Existence.

Contravening natural law is no offense under orthodox statutes, but it is a crime against human potential. The Three Marks of Existence convey a simple blueprint that respects natural law and meets the needs of the human spirit. Impermanence says, "This will pass"; unsatisfactoriness says, "Let go"; and no-self says, "There is no 'me' or 'mine' to cling to." Rather than just algebra and geological formations, if our children were taught these life lessons at school, perhaps real change could be possible in our next generation. In minds schooled in the reality of the human spirit, conflict, extremism, and competition would no longer solve the political sum of our hearts, and our problems would be eased by solving the suffering we chase with our minds.

Moreover, it should go without saying that societies should design and institute social systems supporting the alleviation of suffering rather than stockpiling it for corporate profit. The solutions to your suffering are currently a marketplace of goods and experiences we have created. What madness! Or should I call it *made-ness*! In much the same way that twenty-first-century society now warns people about harmful substances like tobacco, trans fats, or sugar, one day—and I hope that it's one day soon—people will be warned of the great spiritual harm perpetuated by ego, desire, and selfishness, and our society can stop trying to manufacture its way out of the human condition.

Yes, spiritual growth is a personal responsibility, but society has a duty to conform its structures to reality, not to the greedy aspirations of a few puffed-up egos. We now commune in a globalized culture that transmits the propaganda of suffering. It clouds the path of human potential with false promises of future happiness, in a future world that can never exist.

It is not so much that *every* individual would choose the spiritual path were it presented to him or her as an option, but it is not the role of society to make that choice for us. Quite the opposite. The duty of society is to create opportunity. No one should be denied the knowledge of nature's simple truth. No one should be refused the opportunity. *Your* power should be *your* choice.

Today, a society of true spiritual freedom is a dream, but it was once the reality of nomadic tribes who told mythical tales of the rampant ego and the troubles it augured. We live in an age where the spiritual potential of our species has been subjugated to the rank of vassal under state control, but in reality, the game of life is very simple. It is to discover where suffering comes from and to end it. We have the process to do this. We have the method. And we have had that method for thousands of years.

The only question is, why have we not yet done it?

Chapter 8

Defilements

In *Dhammic Socialism*, Buddhadasa nailed down exactly why CLD has not worked and will never work as an effective social foundation. Indeed, accusations of Buddhist spiritual idealism are turned on their head as he skewers, in one Dhammic concept, the naivety that underpins the CLD model:

> It is precisely the problem of *defilements* that make capitalist liberal democracy impractical as anything but an *ideal*. By nature, *people give in to their defilements*. As a consequence, "capitalist liberal democracy" tends to be interpreted in terms of our own selfish, egotistic interests and not the good of the whole.[1]
> (my emphasis)

According to Dhamma, defilements are mental phenomena that debase human potential and stunt spiritual development. They take the form of emotions, so a good metaphor is a bowl of water with the muddy sediment of defilements settled at the bottom. If the bowl remains still, the water will remain clear. But if the bowl is shaken or stirred, the water becomes cloudy and impenetrable.

Defilements like fear, loathing, jealousy, and rage have silently accumulated in all our minds. During traumatic experiences, our world is shaken and the sediment of emotion rising up from our unconscious mind clouds those events. In this mode, we are blinded by these feelings and cannot see reality for what it is. Instead, we evaluate the situation through the mist of the ego, based upon misconceptions and false assumptions.

Emotion is inherent in the human condition. It is part of what it means to be human. But it has a deeper significance than simply feeling either good or bad inside us. Helping people perceive and handle emotion wisely is crucial to cultivating a better life and a happier society. Without this simple wisdom, we become victims of external events, which may cause us to react wildly, without awareness of, or care for, the world around us and the other people in it, and that's bad for everyone.

In fact, defilements are *conditioned mental states* dependent on *three factors*. Let's review these factors before discussing how to overcome them.

1. Spiritual ignorance

Don't get offended by this, but we're all ignorant! Spiritual wisdom is nothing to do with conventional intellect. It is all about, as Buddhadasa used to say, "knowing what is what."

Most global problems are not caused by knowledge deficiency but by defilements. The desire to feed reputation, wealth, or material comforts stems from ignorance, which is a *trained* mental state. We condition this. We make it real. The solution to our global or personal problems is not material. Ignorance reinforces the unconscious repetition of beliefs. This can only be overcome by learning and *practicing* sufficient self-awareness to identify mental defilements and removing their root causes.

Buddha taught meditation for this very reason. In its basic form, meditation observes the illusion of self arising and falling in the present moment. Imagine being able to observe how your emotional reactions have become automated and habitualized. It would be quite shocking to realize how little you knew about yourself, wouldn't it? Indeed, if you practice, you will observe how three phases play out in your mind: when your senses make contact with an event; how your mind classifies the event as good or bad; and your reaction to that event in words and actions.

Each of these three phases presents an opportunity to stop your trained and automated response. If you study them, it will become demonstrably true to you that you have not been in control of your reaction but your reality is a product of it. In short, your defilements are creating and recreating your reality based upon the predefined conditioning of your ego.

This implies that removing the defilement of ignorance is more than learning new things. Even studying the Three Marks of Existence, or the three mental causes of defilements, will not help. While we continue to perceive our worldly problems as a matter of expertise and knowledge, much of this is actually spiritual ignorance. This is how defilements have taken over the world. We don't even know they are there. And we have embraced how they temporarily make us feel.

2. Attachment

From ignorance arises attachment. This mental condition clings to situations, people, or experiences as permanent possessions. It creates the illusion of selfhood through thoughts, feelings, and objects being I, me, or mine. When these attachments are threatened, we cling to them like life rafts, holding on to them as if they are essential parts of ourselves. This is a mere illusion of the mind.

There are many different types of attachments. It may be your attachment to peace and quiet, a drink you enjoy, or a sports team. It could be a loved one, a significant photo, or a memento of a special event. Or it might be an idea, opinion, or thought. However, all attachments, regardless of their type, have the same effect. When a situation changes unexpectedly, your attachment manifests emotion. Disappointment, sadness, fear, or a sense of loss: when the bowl of water gets shaken, the sediment at the bottom of the bowl clouds everything.

Again, this reaction may seem very normal and natural, which it is. No one is saying that you shouldn't feel deeply about what happens to your family or your car or your football team, and so on! It is more about finding a middle path, a balance between enjoying the fruits of this Earth while recognizing that there is a higher purpose to life than making our fruit bowl as big as we possibly can!

A good analogy would be enjoying a night out. We should all be able to let our hair down once in a while. But hopefully, we won't go so far that we trash a bar, steal a car and, you know, destroy a rainforest or two. That kind of thing. But that's what defilements can do. They can cloud the mind until the immoral becomes normal. In ignorance, our attachment to possessions grows stronger than the morality that moderates our behavior. Desire trumps wisdom, and our world becomes profane.

So, yes, defilements are natural, but no, they are not *who you are*. When you are a slave to them, they create suffering; but when you understand and master them, they behave. Like all potentialities, you can pander to their extremes, or you can tame, manage, and control them so they don't get out of hand. Indeed, this practice does not just make good logical sense; it is the key to your spiritual evolution.

The core point is this: we are all spiritually ignorant to some extent, and this ignorance leads to profound physical and mental consequences, such as sleepless nights, conflicts with others, depression, sickness, self-loathing, and can even culminate in acts of violence, for example. Attachments are as much a blight on society as cancer or dementia; moreover, they should be treated as such because they are eminently *preventable*. If people were taught that the multitude of potential issues in their mind, body, and spirit hailed directly from preventable mental defilements, our world could transform. We could move from being a pharmaceutically dependent culture that covers up symptoms, to be a spiritually evolved society that utilizes practical, simple solutions to a natural problem.

3. The desire for more or less

Imagine defilements as a natural subroutine inside your mind's operating system. As your personal OS completes tasks throughout the day, all your experience is filtered through the subroutine of defilements, running quietly under the surface, prompting your ego to react and respond depending on the stimulation.

This defilement subroutine is enormously influential. It wants what it wants and, by demanding its needs are met, the energy to serve other priorities within the greater OS is affected. Thus, the *whole* OS begins to be shaped by thoughts, feelings, and actions influenced by a selfish subroutine.

In simple terms, this subroutine is *desire*. Desires build attachments, and these attachments shake up the sediment from the bowl of your mind. As events in your life unfurl, your desires demand two responses from you: *more* or *less*. You either want to sustain that situation because you enjoy it, or end that situation because you don't.

An example scenario would be a man and his car. He is very attached to his vehicle. He's proud of it. His general belief is that the car brings him joy and convenience. But, like us all, at the root of this attachment is spiritual ignorance. He doesn't see how his desires also cause him great suffering.

This is nothing abnormal. There's nothing intrinsically *wrong* with the man's intention. He has the same aspirations as you and me. He wants to maintain his car in good order and protect his investment because he is afraid to lose or devalue it. What's wrong with that? Nothing. From the spiritual angle, however, we see how cunning our desires are. They convince us that their fulfillment is essential to our wellbeing, which creates a roller-coaster of emotions.

This is reflected in our scenario. The car owner insists on maintaining his car in pristine condition and *worries* that someone will steal or damage it. He gets *angry* when the local kids play football in the street nearby and *hopes* they play somewhere else each evening. His *vanity* has motivated him to customize the car because he wants to feel unique. But it's difficult and *frustrating* to start in the winter, and he fears that one day when it becomes an old banger, he will *hate* it because it looks old and breaks down every 500 miles!

Situations like this play out in all our lives every day. For you, the car in the analogy may be your phone, your job, your home, your clothes, your pet, your bank account, your hair, your partner, and so on. My goodness, attachments are so multitudinous and so deeply ingrained into us all, it could be every single one of these situations and you may not have even noticed!

Ignorance of impermanence, unsatisfactoriness, and no-self transforms reality into illusions. Our motivations are driven by the attachments that cause desires. This feedback loop sustains and legitimizes the false notion that our impulses are synonymous with honest goals or objectives. In reality, most are triggered by defilements that undermine our spiritual potential. When we permit society to cultivate desire, human nature becomes its plaything. To extend our car analogy, we are no longer in the driving seat. The minds that design society are in control.

This is not only mentally draining; it can be fatal. Your emotional responses manifest physical peptides that are released into your body every time you emote.[2] These are known to be the causes of physical issues as serious as cancer. Our mind has the enormous power to transform a tiny mental perception into an actual physical form, regardless of whether it has any foundation in objective reality or not. This is, quite literally, an act of subjective physical creation by the ego, turning a false perception into a physical reality.

***

Society is in denial. It is focused on the impossible dream of manufacturing a global culture that generates enough wealth for all of us to buy our happiness. This doesn't make sense. It is not only destroying the world, everyone *knows* that money is an unnecessary step in the process of happiness. Yes, you need shelter, food, clothing, and so on, the essentials of life, but just consider how much suffering in our materialistic society comes from envy. Marketing plays on our values, self-worth, and natural need for inclusion, manipulating desires to drive trends in society through emotional triggers. In this kind of world, the most important thing you can do is to consume and consume again. What a trap we have made for ourselves!

In reality, life is a simple mathematical equation that states: the less desire you have, the less you will suffer. Your personal fulfillment, not to mention society's spiritual health, is dependent upon *removing the ignorance that underpins desires*. But society has fundamentally misinterpreted this equation as: the more I sate my desires, the less I suffer. In response, we have founded a global reality on manufacturing more things and consuming them. This misinterpretation is gospel. Despite their immense potential to free us, unite us, and build bridges of trust and respect, the many marvels of modern technology such as the Internet, mobile devices, cable TV, virtual reality, and so on, have weaponized defilements and driven them deeper into the collective human psyche. The dreams of everyone, from Almaty to Zurich, are fixated on earning enough money to buy our freedom from the mundane world.

In Osho's *Book of Secrets*, he tells the story of a monk who carries a unique alms bowl. Each day, as is the custom of monks, he passes from home to home in his community, accepting offerings of food and beverages that the locals offer to sustain his ascetic lifestyle. When he passes the home of the richest man in town, the rich man's pride is piqued. He wants to show off. So he brings the monk the finest food from his kitchens and puts it all in the bowl. Weirdly, the bowl does not seem to fill up.

So, the rich man reacts. He orders his servants to bring all the food from his entire larder, which they throw into the alms bowl. But still the bowl remains nearly empty. Intrigued and a little annoyed about this, the rich man retreats to his home once more and returns with servants lugging many huge baskets of jewelry and gems. He throws them all in the bowl, assuming that this will surely fill it to the brim. But still, the bowl remains empty.

Frustrated, the rich man raids his own vaults and retrieves every penny of money and ounce of gold and tosses it into this strange bowl, but still it shows no sign of being even in the slightest bit full. Finally, at his wits' end, and with nothing else to put in, he gets his servants to chop up all his furniture and knock down his house until every piece of equipment and building block from his property is consumed by the bowl too. Now, he has nothing left. But still, the bowl remains ravenous.

When the rich man finally has nothing more to give, he asks the monk how such a bowl is possible. The monk explains that this bowl is no normal alms bowl. It is a human skull and, as we all know, the human skull has such an immense appetite, it can devour the whole world and still ask for more.

This classic Dhammic tale exemplifies the eternal problem of the human mind. It is the same problem every one of us faces. Whatever we have, whatever we create, regardless of the miraculous nature of the technologies and inventions we manufacture, the limitless appetite of the human mind will continue to demand its desires until we challenge it to stop. To feed it endlessly is a forlorn and impossible solution. One mind alone can eat the whole world, several worlds, were we to stand aside and allow it to do so. While it may seem as though our creative culture innovates an endless stream of modern conveniences in a world perpetually progressing, these technologies have been focused on enslaving us in desires, not freeing us from them. This deepens defilements and captures us in a trap of dukkha. Weirdly, the path to freedom and the path to an abundant world where everyone has enough is the same path. It cannot be found in the service of desires but by tempering them so that we all have enough in a society that serves spiritual evolution, not spiritual ignorance.

Buddhadasa spoke of *dependent origination*, which postulates that cause and effect does not happen in sequence but through co-dependence. He used to explain this complex subject in very simple terms, saying: "Because there is this, there is that. And because there is that, there is this." It may be more relatable to you as the infamous chicken and egg riddle, which asks, "Does the chicken or the egg come first?" In Buddhism, the answer is not that one creates the other, but that they both create each other. The existence of one depends on the existence of the other. So how can we say which one was first?

This is the paradoxical nature of profound spiritual truth. If we ponder whether CLD creates beliefs in our minds, or the beliefs in our minds create the CLD, well, dependent origination answers this question. They *create each other*, and this lack of sequence makes it very hard for us to identify the 'first cause' of our unhappiness and remove it. When we enjoy a moment of fun, adventure, excitement, and pleasure, our pain and suffering seem to end. We see the cause and we see the effect, so we keep repeating this pattern. However, dependent origination hides from us how sating desires conditions the mind to desire more, which conditions society to offer more ways to sate desire. In effect, society becomes a self-fulfilling prophecy. Does marketing stimulate desire, or do desires stimulate marketing? Dependent origination suggests they are co-dependent and condition each other.

To turn this around, we need to see the way our mental state not only conditions desires but also sets up our culture to reinforce and proliferate these defilements. Just quickly google the term 'addictive video games' and you'll see what I mean. You'll return a mishmash of results that perfectly characterize the issue. On one hand there will be sites warning of the threats of gaming addiction, and on the other there will be multiple options to download games that urge you to "Download this *addictive* game! It's great!!!!"

This quote from a video addiction site perfectly exemplifies the challenge before us:

Modern video games are a far cry from the games of old. They're no longer just intended to provide a few hours of entertainment. *Gaming companies know exactly how to keep you hooked.* They understand how often to reward you, how to tailor their game to specific people, and how to extract as much money as possible from their players. Video games of today are quite literally *designed to be addictive.*[3]

(my emphasis)

Don't get me wrong. In my life, I have *loved* video games. I've been a player since the ZX Spectrum, but I know firsthand how addictive gaming can be (curse you, Football Manager!). This isn't a rail against the need for us all to take personal responsibility for our choices and it certainly isn't an anti-video-game rant. I wish to paint a bigger picture than that.

I am saying that through the process of dependent origination we have quietly, casually built a society that *requires* addiction and even *values* it at times. Sometimes that is an addiction to a product. Sometimes that is an addiction to making the product and selling it to us. Over the years, the innate dangers of this culture have slowly been identified and addressed by laws that restrict corporations from, for example, selling us cigarettes, plying us with sugar, creating a disposable culture, or polluting the environment. We *know* that some unscrupulous people will take advantage of others, so we adjust the parameters of acceptable society through law.

But what do we do when the entire *psychology* of our culture runs amok and exploits the core impulses of humanity? How do we address the issue when corporations are specifically targeting an increase of defilements as a *win*? In 2017, Shaun Parker, the founder of Napster and the founding president of Facebook, summed up social media by claiming that it "exploit[s] a vulnerability in human psychology" and creates a "social-validation feedback loop." This is a perfect explanation for all products and services that appeal to our fundamental desires. It is not only what social media does. It is not only what video games exploit. It is also what every marketing expert in the world plays upon to create a desirable product. That "vulnerability in human psychology" Parker spoke about has been known for thousands of years. It's called *desire*. And it is a base defilement.

Now, consider that defilements inhibit spiritual evolution in the individual. Place that in the context of a society organized to do exactly that and you begin to perceive the enormous threat to the spiritual evolution of our entire species. Indeed, that same threat is so dangerous, unconscious, and proudly displayed as a benefit, that it can push the entire world to the point of destruction while remaining the root cause of our global problems. The process of dependent origination has produced an external world that is familiar and calming to us because it reflects the mental projections of what we desire and fear most in the world. All around, distractions temporarily delight and engage us while fears motivate us to avoid deeper problems. In principle, there's absolutely nothing wrong with fulfilling desires. Life is about indulgence, experience, and deep, deep feeling. But at the same time, a society that blithely exploits our mental vulnerabilities through its economy is broken. It is unfit for purpose. It is corrupt.

Recognizing our personal defilements takes time. Each of us starts from a position of disbelief. We don't want to believe that we are the victims of our own minds. And we certainly don't want to believe we live in a society that is broken. But we are. And it is. Given 20 minutes to study your own mind, you will see this for yourself. You are not in control of your thoughts. You are not in control of your desires. And, given a few weeks' effort, you could identify how your automated desires and attachments create the world outside. You will see the reality of dependent origination because you will see yourself everywhere you look. Now, ascribe that same tendency to our global leadership and you will see how much of a mess we are in.

The potential payoff of a regular self-inventory is huge. With a little diligence, you can develop the self-control to pause between the moment at which your desires engage and the moment when you react or let it pass. It soon begins to happen just as automatically as you now react and respond. This is not just a little miracle. It is the point when you start climbing the summit of human potential by escaping the automated ego reactions you have cultivated your whole life. Now, the evolution of your character begins. You are on the path to spiritual freedom.

When contemplating a journey of such profound change, many fears arise. You might worry that ending desires would leave you zombified, or that releasing attachments would render your life boring or purposeless. But the opposite is true. In his *Handbook for Mankind*, Buddhadasa said:

Penetrating so far into the real essence of Buddhism... dispels fears, such as the fear that the complete giving up of defilements would make life dry and dreary and utterly devoid of flavor...The victory over all these things is genuine bliss.[4]

It is therefore a great irony that people fear becoming robots if they quell their desires. The reality is literally the opposite. CLD has *already* made us robots. It does not and cannot free us from the bonds that really matter except to demonstrate, in full color and sound, that our existing society is *not* the way. We are trained to automate our ego's reactions, responding to external stimuli with conditioned responses that even go so far as to *encourage* addictions. Society has conditioned us not to cut the ropes that bind us but to find comfort in their embrace. This is not truly living. It is slavery in mental chains.

Undertaking the deconstruction of one's ego is a frightening task, but it is the minimum requirement of a life pursuing spiritual freedom. CLD does nothing to end defilements. It does not warn you of their existence. It peddles an idealistic dream in a fabricated reality that has not existed and will never exist. It is a grade-Λ, gold-standard example of the very ignorance that conditions the root of all desires to have more and to have less. It fails to recognize that every truly social system, regardless of ideological bent, will fail to work for real people if defilements are not acknowledged and addressed as the root cause of all human suffering.

Why? Because as Buddhadasa says, "By nature people give in to their defilements," and any social system that does not deal with the true nature of things or the true needs of people is not a social system at all. It is an invitation to suffer an illusion, quietly, together, alone.

Chapter 9

The Illusion of Progress

All my life I've been told that we live in a time of amazing progress. I've seen the ZX80 morph into the supercomputer; email supersede physical mail; Google make libraries obsolete; wind farms supersede coal-powered plants. So, there's little doubt that amazing *change* is a characteristic of the last 50 years. Like the rest of us, I've marveled at it all. But amid all this transformation, all this wonderment, is humanity really progressing as much as we believe it is?

Progressivism is the idea that history is an unstoppable march towards social improvement. The conventional view perceives it like a graph of exponential growth on a 13,000-year timeline marching in lockstep from the Neolithic Revolution to the emergence of CLD. Since the 1980s, this line shoots upwards into the stratosphere, illustrating the explosive uptick in wealth and technology. *Voilà!* Progress! So we are led to believe.

And what can challenge this intuitive assumption? After all, it's plain to see that twenty-first-century humans have a better life than their forebears living in the Middle Ages, they in turn had it better than the Ancient Greeks, and the Ancient Greeks had it better than prehistoric people living in caves. Right? However, what criteria are used as data for this graph of progress?

One of the great technological symbols of human progress is atomic energy. It is telling that, after the atomic bomb was created, Einstein said: "The release of atomic energy has not created a new problem. It has merely made more urgent the necessity of solving an existing one." He knew perfectly well that neither technologies nor economic growth could address the underlying nature of human beings. Quite the opposite.

They play into the hands of defilements and obscure the risk of building a society shaped by the ego's greatest strengths: humanity's greatest weakness.

We saw in Chapter 3 that *spiritual evolution* is the ultimate measure of human progress. Everything else is a bonus. We've seen that life's purpose is the elimination of suffering and that society has a responsibility to instill in people the knowledge and the skills to eliminate it. Fulfilling this purpose is nothing to do with technology or wealth or anything else that you can measure in conventional terms. But that doesn't mean we can't set benchmarks. In *Dhammic Socialism*, Buddhadasa laid out several criteria for how a spiritual society would be founded:

...living in a socially moral way: acting in the best interests of the entire community by living according to Nature's Laws; avoiding the consumption of goods beyond our simple needs; sharing all that is not essential for us to have with others, even if we consider ourselves poor, giving generously of our wealth if we are well-to-do.[1]

His ideas can be summarized into three criteria:

1. People increasingly living in a socially moral way
2. Society gradually consuming no more than it needs and sustaining this approach once it has attained it
3. And people consistently sharing what they do not need.

Of course, these criteria could be broken down into so-called SMART goals, KPIs (key performance indicators), targets, and objectives, but that's somewhat beyond the remit of this work. What is important to me is the most essential measurement of all: *feelings*. To assert that we truly live in a progressing society, each of us should *feel* all three of these effects in our lives. Today, if you were to go around your community and take a straw poll of your neighbors, would they perceive society as living in an increasingly moral way, consuming no more than it needs, or people sharing what they do not need?

Real progress won't appear on a statistic or a chart. It won't end up on a machine or a digital read-out. The results will resonate in the hearts and minds of people who trust their society *more* today than they did yesterday because it is gradually respecting and supporting their right to live and to pursue liberty from dukkha in a more consistent way. This *sounds* like an abstract gauge because *it is*. Life is abstract! No one can tell you whether you are happy, except *you*. I'd like to see our governments determining the effectiveness of the state, not by GDP or life expectancy, but by quantifying the number of citizens freed from suffering. Now, there's data I could really get behind!

So, we can appraise the progressivist hypothesis by assessing history against Buddhadasa's Three Criteria. If progressivism is true, we should be attaining these three criteria more frequently today than we were in the past. The thing is, when we look back at prehistoric society objectively, we find something rather strange. Instead of the infanticidal, incestuous, anarchic, brutal, insane prehistoric 'cavemen' we were taught about in school,[2] what we find is quite the opposite. Amid a harsh environment and against the backdrop of a treacherous natural world, we find the outline of a spiritual culture sketched out in the form of an amazing social custom.

What we know as the Stone Age is actually three different periods: the Paleolithic, Mesolithic, and Neolithic periods. These span about 2.2 million years and mark the discovery of the earliest stone tools dated by archaeologists up to the beginning of the agricultural age, which is often referred to as the Neolithic (New Stone Age) Revolution. Notably, the Neolithic Revolution coincided with the end of the last ice age and a changing, warmer, more abundant planet.

But let's focus on the twelfth millennium BCE. This was a time just before the Neolithic Revolution and the emergence of the agricultural economy. We are led to believe that life was a brutal, short struggle for survival. Tribes were hunters and gatherers. There were only stone tools. Currency did not exist. Communities are estimated to have numbered between 10 and 50 people. Farming had not been invented. Conditions were unforgiving. And yet, among all this harsh social conditioning where we might assume that a winner-takes-all kind of mentality might reign supreme, there appears a single beacon of cultural light that perfectly exemplifies each of Buddhadasa's Three Criteria.

It is called a *gift economy*. This is a social convention whereby individual tribe members donate their belongings to other people in their tribe as an act of charity. They literally *give away* their possessions. This convention wasn't limited to a few isolated locations. There is a cornucopia of evidence proving that gift economies were commonplace all over the world.

When anthropologists first began to identify gift economies and started researching the intentions of the underlying behavior, they assumed that the primary gifts being donated must have been spoilable goods such as meat, vegetables, or fruit. From the modern perspective, this accorded nicely with our modern value of 'waste not, want not.' It made perfect sense.[3] However, this view soon fell away as, amazingly, gift economies still endure today. And their motivation is far more subtle than 'waste not, want not.' It seems to hint at an overarching set of spiritual values, not unlike Buddhadasa's Three Criteria.

In the 'Moka Exchange' of Papua New Guinea, the 'Potlatch' ceremony of the indigenous peoples of the Pacific Northwest Coast, and the 'Koha' observed by the Māori culture of New Zealand, the gift economy lives on. Moreover, the 'Kula Ring' gift economy from the Milne Bay Province of Papua New Guinea proffers a crucial insight into the values underscoring the process. In this island chain of 18 communities, thousands of people exchange necklaces in a complex ritual that varies across the archipelago. Gift economies were more than a way to share spoilable goods. There was a powerful social dynamic to them that transcends the material benefits of exchange and reveals a startling truth about prehistory.

Anthropologists now believe that gift economies have existed for more than 90% of the entire chronicle of the modern human.[4] That's about 180,000 years or so, no chump-change in the history of the species! It offers us a sneak-peak at the spiritual architecture of ancient society, its values, and its structure. In the same way that we view Adam's Calendar, the Pyramids of Giza, or Stonehenge as monuments that exemplify the values of the people who built them, the gift economy is no less a testimony. It memorializes the motivations and aspirations of ancestors that would otherwise be obscured by time. More significantly, it also peels back the lid on their state of spiritual maturity.

Were these people attuned to spiritual wisdom? Did they understand the Three Marks of Existence? That would certainly demonstrate their social advancement. When we appraise the gift economy from this perspective, we see that it symbolizes an organized act of dispossession, of interdependence, of sharing — the embodiment of Buddhadasa's Three Criteria. If it really did begin 200,000 years ago, it symbolized a powerful line drawn in the sand. It stated humanity's deepest intention to defeat the pressures of desire and dukkha. It says: "We share." It says: "We commune." It says: "We will live what we believe."

You can imagine the power of that ceremony yourself. If it were you, right now, giving away your most precious possession, how would you feel? Would your most precious possession be your phone, your laptop, your car, or your entire bank balance? Think about what you are most attached to. How would you *feel* about giving that away to someone down the end of your street to demonstrate solidarity with them? Put yourself in that headspace and imagine, just for a second, handing that prized asset away. What emotions would stir in you? How powerful would that feeling be? You might feel sadness for your loss, bitterness that the custom is forcing you to do this, or despondency about your prospects of ever acquiring such an impressive object again. Or then again, you might feel proud to be practicing no-self.

While this moment may feel terrible from one perspective, from another it is profound. It forces you to face yourself, up close and personal. For one day of the year, the state of your ignorance of the Three Marks of Existence would be tested. For those attached to their possessions, a feeling would grip them; they would suffer from their attachment and desire. Each of us would have been forced to dip into the pool of our hidden identity, an identity comprised of accumulated defilements in all their naked glory. These would come alive in your mind, body, and emotions.

And that is amazing! What a great way to reveal what lies concealed within you! Unless you deliberately test yourself in situations that force an honest reaction, how do you really know how much ego has accumulated inside you? It is not the loss of the object that stings. It is your ego *reacting to that loss as if it is losing a piece of its self-identity*.

Like the release valve on a steam engine, a gift economy was a simple way to avoid the potential explosion of ego and selfishness in a tribal situation. In tight-knit nomadic groups of people, it was essential too. An eruption of personal ego in such a finely balanced culture could threaten their very existence. Any outbreak of selfish desire would affect the ability of the whole tribe to cooperate, coordinate, and focus on group activities essential for survival.

Remember Buddhadasa's words as he reflected on the feeling of being immersed in nature? He said:

As we sit here in this forest, surrounded by nature, we feel the calming effects of the natural environment…the embodiment of Nature in a pure, balanced state. Here there is no deceit, no "me/mine" distinctions; they simply do not exist.

Reflecting upon this quote, it is not hard to see how nature's ultimate system of sharing could positively influence a community's social system, is it?

And that is exactly what he meant by it. When we listen to nature and are inspired, we create social systems that emulate its interdependent spirit. In antithesis, when we see those same systems and are frightened by them, we seek to control and destroy them. The gift economy was a response to this inspiration, a manifestation of spiritual truth in action. It memorialized nature's most significant spiritual lesson in a custom that could be passed down through tens of thousands of years of history, from generation to generation, teaching people that same lesson across the millennia: *let go, be humble, travel light!* It was a tutorial for the world, a welcome to Earth, a soft reminder that to live in the physical world, one must not be lured in by the trap of materialism. Indeed, it is a testimony to just how powerful that lesson is that the gift economy still endures to this day.

Now, I'm not saying that the Mesolithic period was all roses and chocolates. And I'm not saying that every gift economy was a picture of charity, love, and selflessness either. Far from it. As contemporary gift economies demonstrate today, people give in to their defilements. It's only natural! Some people would have used gift-giving to gain an advantage. Others wanted to be owed a favor or were virtue-signaling, but my point here is not to claim that prehistory was lovely and everything since then has sucked. Dualistic arguments like the past being good and today being bad are overly simplistic and crude.

What I am suggesting is that, in one way or another, our tribal culture has *always known* the spiritual truth I am discussing in this book. As I proposed in the chapters on how organized religion corrupted spiritual truth, there has always been an intuitive understanding in human culture, an overarching spiritual sentiment that has sought to cork the ego-genie in its bottle. For reasons I will soon explore in this book, our most ancient people, despite all their perceived ignorance and disadvantages compared to a modern person, devised a social custom that is not only essentially quite beautiful and graceful but also wise enough to address humanity's most crucial spiritual issue: defilements! That is not just a credit to their state of mind. It is an *astounding* spiritual accomplishment. By virtue of its very historical existence, a gift economy, driven by Buddhadasa's three criteria for spiritual advancement, is testimony to the deep wisdom that existed in prehistoric times.

Moreover, when we examine the core principles of the gift economy, we realize that its fundamental message is one consistently repeated by spiritual masters across history. For example, when Jesus was asked by a rich ruler how he could attain eternal life, he replied: *"sell all that thou hast*, and distribute unto the poor, and thou shalt have treasure in heaven."[5] (my emphasis)

This sentiment is mirrored in Sikhism:

You will have to abandon the materialistic things you have collected. These entanglements will be of no use to you. You are in love with the things that will not go along with you. You think these things are your friends but in fact these are your enemies. In such confusion, the world has gone astray. The foolish mortal wastes this precious human life. He does not like to see Truth and righteousness. He is attached to falsehood and deception; they seem sweet to him. He loves gifts, but he forgets the Giver.[6]

In Islam, the symbolism is even more powerful:

Woe to every backbiter, slanderer,
who amasses wealth greedily and counts it repeatedly,
thinking that their wealth will make them immortal!
Not at all! Such a person will certainly be tossed into the Crusher.
And what will make you realize what the Crusher is?
It is Allah's kindled Fire...[7]

It is my opinion that gift economies were not naive nice-to-have social customs from an innocent age. They were deliberate, focused, and played an essential role in molding human behavioral psychology. Their core message was clearly stated by Jesus. It was as clear in Sikhism, Islam, or Hinduism as it was in Buddhism. Whether we call material attachments "hell," "the Crusher," or "enemies," the message resonates loud and clear across history—people give in to their defilements and this threatens one's personal spiritual health. Indeed, a society built upon defilements threatens the spiritual evolution of our entire species!

History has not been the smooth straight line from bad to good that progressivism might postulate. Indeed, it would be fairer to describe it as a long tangle between the peaks of the spirit and the troughs of the ego. On occasion, the light has shone and renaissance has broken out. At other times, darkness has fallen and less illuminated ideas have run the world.

While conventional historians will delineate historical periods by a measure of technological prowess (Iron Age, Industrial Revolution, and so on), I want to share with you a different demarcation that begins by answering a simple question: "Who started the gift economy?"

I admit up front, there is no specific answer to this question. There is no single name that can be argued over on Wikipedia. The answer to the question is, in fact, a *phenomenon*. It is what happens within society when a single practitioner starts the spiritual journey and chooses to travel all the way to its end.

This person is such a rarity, so noteworthy, such a bright light, that they have the potential to spark a golden age in their tribe. Their influence teaches their people simple ways to avoid the pitfalls that would otherwise ensnare their society in defilements and ego. For a brief moment in history, they will ignite a cultural renaissance that spurs great achievements in art, science, philosophy, or governance. And, in the most profound of cases, even though their name is forgotten in the mists of time, their teachings may shine across the world for thousands and thousands and thousands of years.

Chapter 10

Golden Ages and Enlightenment

If brain size and intellect are connected, the history of the human brain tells a counterintuitive story. Anthropologists show that the human brain reached its largest volume of 1500ml around *200,000 years ago*. Then, by the time the Neolithic Revolution came around, approximately 190,000 years later, it had *shrunk* to its modern volume of around 1300ml.[1] In other words, our modern brains are 13.3% *smaller* than those of our cave-dwelling ancestors!

Pop! I think that's the sound of our collective egos deflating! However, there's more hot air to release yet. According to scientific studies: "Over the past 30 years and across many parts of the world, there have been significant decreases in IQ, with the largest declines observed in industrialized nations."[2] This statistic alone starkly contradicts our perception of conventional progressivism, doesn't it?

Yet, this gentle decline in human intellect is no shock to the philosophy and writings in civilization after civilization over the millennia of human history. The Greek poet, Hesiod, described five 'Ages of Man': Gold, Silver, Bronze, Heroic, then Iron. He penned this idea in his book, *Works and Days*, circa 700BCE. From these thoughts, modern society has adopted his theory of Golden Ages. But what is truly remarkable about Hesiod's Ages of Man is that it describes these ages as gradually following a pattern of *decline*. Humanity starts with a Golden Age, and then things deteriorate.

If this depressing vision of historical decline had been uniquely Hesiod's, we might be forgiven for dismissing it as poetic fantasy. But it wasn't. In fact, Hinduism reflects this very phenomenon in a pattern of ages called 'yugas.' One entire cycle of ages extends over 4,320,000 years and is comprised of four different yugas.

The first was the Satya Yuga, which is the purest age of all. Hindus know this as the age of truth, a time in ancient history when gods governed the Earth, ruled by Dhamma, symbolized by a bull. However, as each cycle passes, the bull loses a leg, until we arrive at the present age, the Kali Yuga, the most demeritorious age of them all. It is an age where spiritual development has been lost and humanity has been debased. After all, there's not much you can achieve with a legless bull!

Readers will note how this pattern of spiritual decline very much reflects Buddhadasa's warnings and the philosophical premise of this book. Human beings are driven by desires and attachments, and history reflects this accumulation of spiritual ignorance. We shouldn't be surprised that this pattern of deterioration has been known, recorded, and hinted at by all our spiritual legacies. The entire history of this Earth is essentially a spiritual odyssey that awakened people have had access to for thousands of years. When we live in natural, interdependent, symbiotic environments, our nomadic minds are entrained to tap in to this reality, talk about it, and warn our tribes to seek selfless impermanence, not materialistic attachments.

But they always knew this would be a losing battle. We human beings give in to our defilements. And, as the shifting social dynamics built burgeoning cities and competitive economies, the selfish ego flourished in a social environment perfectly predisposed to its nourishment. Through novel social systems, conventions, ideas, and values, a subtle hierarchy of ego was established that eroded the natural order of tribal life that had existed for hundreds of thousands of years and, in its place, established an order of spiritual ignorance through competition.

As competition took root, egalitarianism broke down and the ego became more dominant. As each 'age' of man brings decline, the next age is less evolved than the last, and more architecture of the ego is constructed. This trend increasingly disconnects society and people from natural Dhamma that once entrained us in the patterns of the Three Marks of Existence. Spiritual truth is slowly denigrated and ridiculed until, eventually, the shapes and patterns of ego strangle the spiritual potential of humanity. Like a thief in the night, the ego has won and we don't even know it.

However, there is a secondary phenomenon at work that is highly significant to acknowledge and explore. In *We-Topia* thus far, we have examined history in terms of spiritual development and in terms of conventional notions of progressivism. If we were to plot these two phenomena on a single graph, the trend of spiritual development would point down and the trend of conventional progressivism would point up.

However, these two lines would not point straight, either one way or the other. Occasional peaks of progress or troughs of decline would interrupt each, representing how the different regions of the world have gone through slumps or revivals. While there exists a general trend in both those plotted lines, as technical prowess grew across the globe and spiritual wisdom diminished, within those trends, we find peculiar and intriguing historical peaks that interrupt the general trend. What were these exciting moments in history where, for a century or more, sometimes several centuries, spiritual decline was arrested *and* technical prowess accelerated in partnership with one another?

These are what can be termed as 'mini Golden Ages.' They flare up like beacons of revival from the cinders of decay. They mark a great contrast between the dying of old ways and a few short, extraordinary centuries during which a strange and beautiful kind of intelligence rekindles and reminds us all of the deeper potential of human spirituality. As these Golden Ages burst into life across history, the cooling embers of a region's spiritual purpose are stirred back to life, a renaissance, igniting social cohesion through art, culture, philosophy, and invention in ways that illuminate the spirit and imprint its mark indelibly on the seal of history.

Ancient Egypt energized Africa and the Mediterranean; Ancient Greece inspired European culture; the Gupta Empire united India; the Chinese Han Dynasty shone in East Asia; Assyria exploded with life in the Middle East: these and many other such epochs of history have left an indelible impression on the whole planet, proudly stamping their mark on the collective psyche of our species today. What sets them apart is not just the art, architecture, or economy of those places, but the values they stood for, the notion that humanity could *do* better, *be* better, and *aspire higher*.

From these epochs came such profound ideas that they forged our world today. In philosophy alone we can still see today the effects of Ptahhotep of Egypt, Plato of Greece, Cyrus II of Persia, Laozi of China, Marcus Aurelius of Rome, and concepts like the Theory of Forms, cuneiform writing, the heliocentric view of the Earth revolving around the sun,[3] Confucianism, and others. My point is to merely illustrate the phenomenon of Golden Ages and their profound effect on history. Indeed, we can even speculate that the gift economy was a product of this phenomenon, an enduring illumination in history that held back the creeping darkness.

Some might claim that such Golden Ages are mere coincidences, a peculiar confluence of talent and opportunity at key moments in history, but I beg to differ. These are not random collisions of intelligence, spirit, and attitude at a nondescript time and place. On the contrary, I suggest that they have determinable triggers that we can identify as clear as day. To do that, let's just step back a moment and ask a connected question. We have looked at the Three Marks of Existence and the causes of defilements and claimed that, if a person can end the desires that create attachments, their spiritual journey will be complete. They will have achieved life's purpose. But what actually *happens* when a person frees themselves from attachments? What is the result?

In Buddhism, this ultimate spiritual truth is called *nirvana* (enlightenment). One who has achieved this state is called an *arahant*, which means 'one who is worthy,' and the word comes from its Pali root meaning: 'to deserve.' It is crucial to understand that enlightenment is not so much a fixed point on a journey but more a gradual realization that eventually becomes so powerful it cannot be resisted.

The idea that a no-self practitioner *achieves enlightenment* is therefore quite misleading, for enlightenment is better analogized as a spectrum of consciousness along which a person slides through practice. The spiritual masters whom we build entire religions around are very obvious examples of people achieving a high degree of spiritual liberation during their lifetime, but many, many others attain this under the radar of public recognition. They may be perceived as artistic, scientific, compassionate, or focused, for example. When a person reaches the point of being an arahant, this is the highest point on the spectrum, the point of no return. The person removes themselves from the cycle of life and death because they have conquered every trigger of defilement that binds them to physically manifest their ego in corporeal form. *This* is completing the journey of life: enlightenment.

From the perspective of *We-Topia*, there is no greater society than one that promotes the conditions for its citizens to discard defilements and become an arahant. I previously lived in Thailand for many years, and one of the finest achievements of its culture is nurturing the social conditions where this is encouraged. Its Buddhist values highlight the merits of detachment, the perils of defilements, and the path to liberty. For the entire history of the country, over 700 years, men and women have been ordained into a Buddhist sangha, and laypeople have supported that community through alms-giving. In this way, the sangha is like an enduring gift society all of its own. Generations of this system have produced arahants of great repute such as Ajarn Chah, Lung Por Poo, Ajarn Mun, Lung Por Tuad and not forgetting Ajarn Buddhadasa himself. Of course, most of these names have passed silently under the radar of all but the most inquiring Western minds because our culture has little interest in higher spiritual attainment. Meanwhile, within Thailand, the reputations of these devout practitioners ring long, loud, and resolutely within the memories of Thai Buddhists who revere them all to this day.

Indeed, since Thailand's inception, such figures have sparked multiple mini Golden Ages that demonstrate the great social power of cultivating spiritual minds that can liberate people around them. All over the Buddhist world, there are similar stories, from Japan to China and India, showing how the intention of building a society focused on releasing desires and attachments fashions a community of people freed from the ego. And, when this liberty occurs in groups of people, or through a single person perfectly liberated, this has a profound impact on society at large. Like shining a bright light into a dark tunnel, the effect of enlightened people cannot help but illuminate the lives of all those attracted to the light.

In my mind, *enlightenment*, the process in which people attain a *higher degree of liberty from selfhood*, is the missing ingredient that explains the peaks and troughs of history. It explains that Golden Ages are limited periods of time in which minds, pregnant with potential, embrace and exercise a high degree of enlightenment. It also explains why, over the great expanse of human history, these brighter moments of illumination have become less and less frequent. As our degrading spiritual society has increased defilements, the conditions for enlightenment have become less and less nurturing. And, as our world has become more globalized, local cultures that were once insulated from selfish ideas are now affected by the same global influences that prescribe material possessions as the cure for our spiritual deficiencies.

Tens of thousands of years ago, our ancient ancestors were already doing what most of us today would find hard or even impossible to do. They were living in gift economies, enjoying a life that routinely divested themselves of the attachments that cause dukkha. They lived in highly sophisticated societies where people naturally looked after each other, organized to address their physical, mental, and spiritual needs. Indeed, this format of culture was so advanced that they freely provided their citizens with every opportunity to evolve to the highest spiritual states attainable on Earth.

What an incredible achievement this was! It didn't rely on wealth or technology. It occurred in some of the poorest areas of the world and resulted in some of the most fundamental and long-lasting developments in human culture. However, as we are well aware, other than in remote regions, ideas like the gift economy did not survive. The impetus was lost. This kind of development was abandoned as a social goal. Indeed, the egalitarian, spiritually evolved society, highly effective at manifesting no-self, was *renounced* in favor of a social system that divided us into classes, reduced personal power, and obscured the potential of humanity.

Indeed, over time, everything that I have described as being essential for the realization of no-self and spiritual wisdom was eroded, demeaned, and eventually forsaken. It's time to answer the biggest question of them all: What was the spark that ended the spiritual age of the nomadic human? And why, as the Hindus predicted, did humanity step over the edge and into the final and most demeritorious age of man: the Kali Yuga?

Chapter 11

The Neolithic Revolution

Modern history paints the advent of agricultural society as an almost exclusively positive innovation. So the accepted theory goes, without agriculture, humanity could never have attained today's civilized society. Indeed, open any history book on the subject and everyone agrees: nomadism was unrelenting "Urgh!" and agriculture was unmitigated "Wow!"

> Without agriculture, it is not possible to have a city, stock market, banks, university, church or army. Agriculture is the foundation of civilization and any stable economy.
> **Allan Savory** — Zimbabwean biologist and environmentalist

> Agriculture not only gives riches to a nation, but the only riches she can call her own.
> **Samuel Johnson** — English writer

> The discovery of agriculture was the first big step toward a civilized life.
> **Arthur Keith** — Scottish anatomist and anthropologist

That's a lot of love. Cities, stock markets, armies, wealth, and freedom: this vast bounty of modern riches encapsulates the conventional perception of what the Neolithic Revolution eventually bequeathed to modern human beings. So the story goes, without this quantum leap in technology and skill-set, humanity might still be stuck back in the bad old days of a hand-to-mouth existence and flint technology...

So the story goes.

The Neolithic Revolution was more than just a revolution in how we fed ourselves. It was a cultural trade-off that changed everything we thought, felt, and believed about the natural order too. Counterintuitively, this so-called "first big step toward a civilized life" was a huge step *backward* in food productivity, nutrition, and health. It negatively impacted human wellbeing for thousands of years. Indeed, it was the single biggest influence on establishing the most demeritorious age humankind has ever known.

That sounds almost unbelievable. But it's true. In May 1987, *Discover* magazine published an article by the noted American geographer and author Jared Diamond, entitled 'The Worst Mistake in the History of the Human Race.' In his article, Diamond refutes every assumption made about sedentary agricultural life point by point. He agrees that the advent of agriculture was a stunning moment in history, but not stunning in the way that one takes a family photograph and proudly displays it on the mantelpiece! What Diamond meant by 'stunning' was more the kind of thing that shocks the hell out of you, gets stuffed into the back of the kitchen drawer, and is never spoken of again!

However, Diamond freely acknowledges the mass public resistance to this idea, agreeing that equivocation on the benefits of farming seems argumentative and inane:

From the progressivist perspective on which I was brought up, to ask "Why did almost all our hunter-gatherer ancestors adopt agriculture?" is silly. Of course they adopted it because agriculture is an efficient way to get more food for less work. Planted crops yield far more tons per acre than roots and berries. Just imagine a band of savages, exhausted from searching for nuts or chasing wild animals, suddenly grazing for the first time at a fruit-laden orchard or a pasture full of sheep. How many milliseconds do you think it would take them to appreciate the advantages of agriculture?[1]

Yet, the problem with the whole progressivist viewpoint that Diamond himself makes in that paragraph is the tiny matter of *evidence*. Diamond argued that prevailing academic opinions of the time were more a product of confirmation bias than empirical data. Researchers believed in progressivism, so they found ideas that supported it. Before technologies like radiocarbon dating became commonplace in the 1950s, much of prehistory was defined by personal extrapolation, experience, and opinion, and much of that opinion was led by the loudest voices. We wanted to believe that life as a nomad was hellish and brutal, so that's how we framed our loudest references to it!

However, one source of evidence has survived and it hails from the most reliable source of all: there are still tribes in the world whose lifestyle has barely changed in the last 200,000 years. All we had to do was ask them, and Diamond's paper did just that:

It turns out that these people have plenty of leisure time, sleep a good deal, and work less hard than their farming neighbors...the average time devoted each week to obtaining food is only 12 to 19 hours for one group of Bushmen, 14 hours or less for the Hadza nomads of Tanzania. One Bushman, when asked why he hadn't emulated neighboring tribes by adopting agriculture, replied, "Why should we, when there are so many mongongo nuts in the world?"[2]

Hold on! Hunting and foraging for food are *more* productive than farming and it requires *less* effort? Who'd've thunk it? And the more the preconceptions of the nomadic life are questioned, the more they are shown up for what they are: *false assumptions*.

A second assumption we often make is that farming was an innovation in health and nutrition too. Sadly, quite the opposite is true:

...the Bushmen's average daily food intake (during a month when food was plentiful) was 2,140 calories and 93 grams of protein, considerably greater than the recommended daily allowance for people of their size. It's almost inconceivable that Bushmen, who eat 75 or so wild plants, could die of starvation the way hundreds of thousands of Irish farmers and their families did during the potato famine of the 1840s.[3]

But there's more. The science of paleopathology (the study of diseases in the bones of skeletal remains) reveals even more shocking counterintuitive evidence.

Skeletons from Greece and Turkey show that the average height of hunter-gatherers toward the end of the ice ages was a generous 5' 9" for men, 5' 5" for women. With the adoption of agriculture, height crashed, and by 3000 B.C. had reached a low of only 5' 3" for men, 5' for women...modern Greeks and Turks have still not regained the average height of their distant ancestors.[4]

Even in relatively modern times, the impact of adopting the agricultural lifestyle has been disastrous for nomadic tribes. In the Native American culture, 800 skeletons were excavated to reveal eye-watering implications:

Compared to the hunter-gatherers who preceded them, the farmers had a nearly 50 per cent increase in enamel defects indicative of malnutrition, a fourfold increase in iron-deficiency anemia...a threefold rise in bone lesions reflecting infectious disease in general, and an increase in degenerative conditions of the spine, probably reflecting a lot of hard physical labor. "Life expectancy at birth in the pre-agricultural community was about twenty-six years," says Armelagos, "but in the post-agricultural community it was nineteen years.

So these episodes of nutritional stress and infectious disease were seriously affecting their ability to survive."[5]

This is damning evidence. From a nutritional perspective, the agricultural lifestyle directly led to shorter lives, smaller people, and less healthy diets. Can there really be more? Yes, there can.

...the mere fact that agriculture encouraged people to clump together in crowded societies, many of which then carried on trade with other crowded societies, *led to the spread of parasites and infectious disease*...Epidemics couldn't take hold when populations were scattered in small bands that constantly shifted camp. *Tuberculosis and diarrheal disease had to await the rise of farming, measles and bubonic plague the appearance of large cities.*[6]

(my emphasis)

After the Neolithic Revolution, the context of human life was forever altered. *Something* changed, and that 'something' can be defined as a shift in the core values of our species. While nomadic life is rooted in a world of possessionless chaos, the sedentary community is organized around an ideology of *accumulation* and *control*. To till the land, you must first possess and defend it. This establishes the idea that you possess those crops, *and* the surrounding buildings, *and* an ever-extending perimeter of land, and so on. This paradigm of possession had an incredibly potent effect on the mentality of these new farmers. For the first time, humanity sees the potential beyond the *temporary* use of a bush or tree or other food sources. We bought into the illusion that humankind can *permanently possess* nature. We jumped down the rabbit hole of an illusion. We succumbed to a lie that had been knocking on the door of our consciousness since humanity first walked on the planet: to control our fears we must control the scary natural world.

Readers will note that possession and control directly conflict with the laws of no-self, impermanence, and unsatisfactoriness, so this period of transition also marks a glaring shift away from the spiritual values of the selfless gift economy and towards the 'me' economy, where possession begins to define personal identity.

Moreover, the rational premise for the paradigm of possession and control that the world subscribes to today is that it provides more efficient, productive security than nomadism. But the evidence seems to contradict this. Indeed, in describing the Neolithic Revolution, Diamond pulls no punches. He frames it as "a catastrophe from which we never recovered."

Of course, humanity cannot go back to a nomadic existence and no one is suggesting we should. However, the gathering evidence is profound enough to cause us to question the global identity of our species that we accept and embrace as normal today. The remarkable conclusion is that, 13,000 years ago, sedentary society began to stratify society and inhibit the most invaluable freedom of tribal members in ways that were unthinkable during the many, many millennia of nomadic tribalism. Individual and tribal identity began to diverge and personal, ego-driven objectives became more plausible. For the first time in history, the identity of each tribal member was being shaped, not by the collective values of the tribal community, but by individual desires that drove the accumulation of personal material possessions within an emerging social hierarchy.

Arthur Keith described the Neolithic Revolution as "the first big step toward a civilized life," but I would call it the first step toward *the great illusion*. We had let loose the dogs of ego, the desires of our inner nature, our competitive self, and its appetite for endless consumption. From this foundation, our entire civilization was founded on personal power and possessions. Individualism *became essential*. And 'making a name for oneself' *appeared* to manufacture a permanent identity for our self. But it doesn't. It never has. It's all myth that only appears real in a world we have conjured up in our heads.

Moreover, as the Neolithic Revolution became the new normal in the world, we were left with something of a paradox, a paradox that needs an answer. Farming is less efficient, less productive, and less healthy than nomadism, yet our modern world clearly shows that humanity *chose* this lifestyle over an easier, freer, more egalitarian social structure. Why did we do that? How did that kind of trade-off ever make sense? Because, on the face of it, we traded a laissez-faire, hammock-swinging lifestyle for back-breaking early morning rises and clearing out pig pens. It doesn't compute.

Not yet, anyway.

To fully understand how agriculture took off, we need to put a couple more of ego's chess pieces in play. You see, farming was just the first in a long historical line of competitive systems by which the fruits of this new competition would be divvied up. To the victor, the spoils. But what we didn't know at the time was that the victors in this new world would need to win a war not just against the might of physical armies. This victory could only be won by establishing an entire mental paradigm that would grab the world by the scruff of its neck and keep repeating the biggest lie of the lot: *the truth is measurable.*

Chapter 12

Spiritual Wisdom versus Practical Truth

Remember all those Hollywood caveman movies where the dominant men head off to the hunt as their female partners dutifully tend to the home? A study conducted with the still flourishing Aeta tribe in the Philippines found that 85% of hunts are led by women and the success rate of all-women hunts is 14% better than that of their male counterparts.[1] Whoops!

It turns out that our assumptions about life in a hunter-gatherer society have more to do with modern biases than the actual culture of our ancient tribal ancestors. Indeed, the erroneous assumption that prehistoric life was hierarchical and misogynistic was put to bed by Mark Dyble, an anthropologist from University College London when, in 2015, Dyble led a study into equality in prehistoric societies and stated conclusively: "it was only with the emergence of agriculture, when people could start to accumulate resources, that inequality emerged."[2] Furthermore, the book *The Creation of Patriarchy*, by Gerder Lerner, links the roots of patriarchy to a period as far back as 8000BCE, a few thousand years after agriculture and the sedentary community became nigh-on universal.

From the perspective of We-Topia, this draws us to an uncomfortable conclusion: the origins of agriculture and inequality are causally linked. Moreover, having already established that both these phenomena were the products of accumulating social ego, we begin to realize that the Neolithic Revolution was far more than a dramatic shift in nutrition. It was the origin of a psychological transformation that *recalibrated human values* until inequality, elitism, and a hierarchy of human significance and merit became conventional.

Gerder Lerner suggested that, sometime between 11,000 and 6000 years ago, *patriarchy* emerged. By the time history arrived at the fifteenth century CE, this effect was brutal. The fifteenth-century monk, Martin Luther, defined his view of women with astounding clarity: "The word and works of God is quite clear, that women were made either to be wives or prostitutes." By the nineteenth century, things had gotten even worse. Napoleon Bonaparte said: "Nature intended women to be our slaves. They are our property." And by the *twentieth century*, Norman Mailer coined the jaw-dropping phrase: "A little bit of rape is good for a man's soul."

In short, movements like the women's suffrage movement in the twentieth century and the Me Too movements in the twenty-first century are not establishing equality and rights for the first time. They are *reestablishing* rights that were eroded thousands of years ago when the stratification of our societies around the world became normalized. To explain how the role of women in society performed a psychological flip from *gender equality* to *male property*, we need to do a little more than simply identify the historical events that hastened this effect. We must prise open the vault of human psychology and ponder this phenomenon as a symptom of a deeper malaise, a spiritual ignorance that prevents modern people from grabbing the nettle of consciousness once again and rebooting our spiritual evolution. If we want to evolve, we have to understand what stopped us, why those hindrances are still in effect, and what we have to change to bring We-Topia to life.

Broken down into its simplest form, life is a series of choices. You, me, everyone: we make our choices by discerning good from bad, right from wrong, kind from mean, and so on. But our parents, religion, schools, culture, and society heavily influence this system of discernment. From birth, our minds are programmed with values that have been passed down to us from our forebears, automatically sorting the world into binary opposites of right *or* wrong, good *or* bad, kind *or* mean.

This dualistic sorting system chops reality up into manageable chunks, but it is also incredibly reductive. There's no subtlety or nuance to it. The mind embraces one idea (right) and excludes all others (wrong), and we file these conclusions away as part of our identity. We can then fight for those things that sit in our camp or fight against those people who sit in the other. It gives us our sense of outrage or conceit when we judge others who sit beyond the scope of our neat little dichotomy.

This is a great way to build ego, but a poor way to build a closer connection to what's real. When we believe that the world is really split into two sides, our mind begins to create the world that simplistic way. After all, dualism is logical, so it seems like we are using a reliable thinking system. In such a system, dualism either exists or it doesn't! And, if it exists (which we were told at school that it certainly does), the mind resists filing ideas/concepts/values as *slightly* right or *slightly* wrong, or *both* very good *and* a little bad. In the *system* we have been taught, that nuance doesn't make much sense.

But this is not reality. In the real world both good and bad have gradients. That's why we don't execute people for lying or let them off with a warning for murder. There are shades of goodness and shades of badness, and the discerning mind learns to make a fair judgment on them because, well, it's far more *real*.

We embrace dualism because, superficially, it seems to be a better survival tool. It's natural and it's fast. Research suggests we make judgments on people in one tenth of a second.[3] What more do we need than a system that is easily remembered, and quickly recalled when we need to respond to it? After meeting a new person, object, or situation for the first time, we judge it, label it, and file it away. Then, when we next meet that person, object, or situation, our past judgment is available for quick access, reducing reaction times in a life-or-death pinch. This is a great way to organize threat levels. We already know that a tiger is dangerous (run away), friends are safe (relax), and chocolate is tasty (give me more!).

However, we *also* know that clinging to the notion that our selfhood is constantly under threat is unhealthy. Indeed, it is absolutely the opposite of what human evolution prescribes. No-self accepts that everything in nature is impermanent, including our own physical life. This does not mean that you should saunter casually towards that marauding tiger, should you happen upon such a beast during your Sunday stroll through Tamworth or wherever. It does mean that we should all learn to recognize our fears for what they usually are: temporary illusions of threat that originate more from our ego's need to preserve itself than they do from the actual scale or reality of the threat.

These impulses are examples of *aversion*. You will note that aversion is simply the inverse of desire. Just like desires, they are survival impulses that stem from the oldest part of the human brain, the reptilian brain, around which the more subtle emotional and thinking brains are wrapped. Developing self-awareness attunes you to the frequency with which your mind defaults into a reactive state. You learn to perceive the feeling that precedes your reaction for what it is, an illusion. Then, you train your mind to feel the emotion pass through it without clinging to the idea that 'something is happening to me' or 'I am losing/gaining something I want/don't want.' Over time, this resets the triggers you have trained into your psychology. The mind calms and you take more control of your feelings and responses.

However, the tendency of people to overreact to threat, our naturally wary disposition, is one of the primary ways in which society manipulates its population. We are much more likely to remember and react to a negative motivation than a positive one. Indeed, people will more readily believe that a negative outcome was a deliberate act, as opposed to a positive one. This tendency is called *negativity bias*. Our minds are trained to recall negative events more strongly than positive ones; therefore we develop this natural aversion to them. Moreover, it is understandable that our minds are well inculcated into this prevailing way of thinking when our daily lives are bombarded by bad news and sickening stories of people we trust doing bad things.

Don't you ever feel as though you're being manipulated into seeing the world through a filter that you didn't create but surely participate in? At the end of the day, there is a mountain of scientific evidence that shows how the human mind works, and those who are best at manipulating social opinion are those who know this better than you. We need only repeat the quote from Shaun Parker, the founder of Napster and founding president of Facebook, to know this is true. Social media, he said, "exploit[s] a vulnerability in human psychology" and creates a "social-validation feedback loop." We are being manipulated, every day, softly, quietly, and most of us assume it is relatively benevolent. But if that results in our enslavement to desire and aversion by default, how benevolent is it in practice?

Yes, our reliance on dualism helps us choose to run away from a tiger, but creating this false dichotomy of the world object by object, person by person, and situation by situation, manufactures a mental conundrum that humanity has thus far failed to solve. The outside isn't fixed. The inside isn't fixed. The outside isn't separate from the inside. And our ideas have nuances, shades, and myriad perspectives. But our mind's artistic brush can annihilate all this beautiful subtlety with one broad sweep when society teaches us to be judgmental and to fall back on the reaction of our reptilian brain. In a sense, we *believe* into reality the notion that dualism exists and it is a fair and reasonable perception of the world.

The accumulation of your experience into absolute truth is exactly the process of learning that adds layer upon layer of myth to your onion-like ego. The thinking that gets you there is completely reductive, but all around the world the majority participate in it because it is simple, saves time, and allows others to do our thinking for us. We like to believe that we are too clever to have the wool pulled over our eyes and yet most of us now get our best ideas from the media, from YouTube, from our mobile apps, and from Tik Tok, all from content creators who have advertisers to serve and political agendas to peddle. This simplifies reality for us into simple right and wrong or good and bad, but when it does this to the point where it no longer represents anything *real*, just what we would like to *believe* is real, it becomes a mere caricature of reality; a fiction that is no more and no less real than a Hollywood movie.

Indeed, if we reflect back upon the three causes of defilements, we will recall that ignorance of reality sits at its root. The absolutes of dualism are core ignorance. It contradicts the *spiritual wisdom* of no-self from the Three Marks of Existence. In fact, nothing has a permanent self or an absolute identity and we should be mindful to challenge anything that claims otherwise.

Sadly, the world is being increasingly fed a diet of dualism. We embrace it, encourage it, and use it like chum to attract sharks into the waters of reasoned debate. Chat forums, TV shows, and social media posts churn with diametrically opposed viewpoints. Yet, it's all for clicks, likes, and subscribes. Even loathing has been monetized. Hatred has a value. Conflict is desirable. We're so busy canceling each other, trolling, and trying to win arguments, that meaningful discussion polarizes into left and right, men and women, rich and poor, positive and negative, pro or anti—and this is very dangerous. This is how we splinter psychologically. This is how different polarities stop perceiving each other as being human or having equal value.

This is how history percolates into unconscionable thoughts and actions justified by people who have lost all perspective on the truth that binds all humanity as one: we all suffer.

The problem we face is an inability to use dualism mindfully. We're either all in or not in at all, but dualism is a double-edged sword. On the one hand, it may be a poor representation of reality but, on the other, it is also indispensable. It underpins all language, ideation, meaning, and organization. It is a *practical truth* that we cannot do without. Just imagine how ridiculous the world would be if you didn't automatically label material objects and recognize what they were the next time you saw them! Imagine if you never made up your mind about ideas you agree with or disagree with. Imagine if you had to form a new opinion of people, each time you met them. The world would not just become confusing and stressful. It would become intolerable.

This paradox between spiritual wisdom and practical truth is one of the greatest known to humankind: the illusion of duality versus the subtle reality of no-self. While the two sides of this paradox seem irreconcilable, in effect, this quandary is like a Zen puzzle *built into the very structure of the universe*. It is a riddle as impossible to answer as "What is the sound of one hand clapping?" How do we live in a dualistic world without unleashing the ego that thrives on dualism?

I believe that this paradox is no coincidence. It is innate within the universe, a law as real as gravity or pressure. It challenges the force of mind, a mind that has only become capable of contemplating this paradox once it has evolved from single-celled life, over billions of years, to the point where but a single creature on this Earth is capable of pondering the question. That creature is the human being. And that mind is the human mind. We are each being challenged to walk a middle path that integrates *both* spiritual wisdom *and* practical truth into one way of life. We are being coaxed to find moderation in all that we do. In effect, the very architecture of our minds challenges us to evolve beyond the reductionism of our reptilian instincts that would trigger us to run away or fight for our lives, and integrate the spiritual wisdom of the Three Marks of Existence and natural Dhamma into how we perceive and interact with the world.

How do we do that? Well, to answer that question with absolute certainty would be an act of dualism in itself, for how can we define a single path when eight billion people start from a different place? The reality is that we need eight billion paths. All I can say is that the process of liberty has certain characteristics that we can all share, certain behaviors that we can all mimic, and certain qualities that we can all explore. The first of these is the *non-judgmental mind*.

Ever since I was a young man seeking truth and absolutes in the foothills of the Indian Himalayas, I've been on a journey of learning non-judgment. I didn't know it at the time. In fact, I went there seeking absolute truth, absolutely sure it existed, and over the decades since I have found relinquishing my hold on a search for the perfect idea to be incredibly difficult. The tool with which I have chipped away at this misconception has been meditation, but for decades I really did not get how or what meditation was. I wanted to approach my meditation with the same dualistic value system that crushed my every attempt to meditate. I sat and judged and criticized and loathed the process because, in my mind, there had to be a win. There had to be a measurable, discernible improvement each time. I lived (and failed) by the philosophy of the right way and the wrong way. If meditation wasn't going to fit into my worldview of truth versus fiction, then meditation was the issue. Or *me*. Or my *lack of skill or technique*. But it was really none of those things. In fact, nothing *really* fits a mind that judges, however useful it may be.

When I sat and *really* studied my mind, I realized that every emotional trauma I have ever suffered was made by judgment.

Judging my past caused sadness. Judging my present caused frustration. Judging my future caused fear. And how do you live happily when your system of discernment *automatically* creates unhappiness? You cannot. It is impossible. You become a robot trapped in a repetitive sequence of cause and effect.

In this reality, it was impossible for me to use meditation for non-judgment when everything in my mind judged my meditation. Every time I got into a pattern of practice, my doubts and self-criticism would surface to sabotage my progress. This went on for 25 years. I was as much an addict of my preexisting thoughts as any alcoholic or drug addict who longs for their high.

But inside me burned that same inquisitive sense of purpose that had inspired me to head to India in the first place. I *knew* there *is* a truth. But I just didn't know that the truth I was looking for was spiritual wisdom. It wasn't dualism. What I really needed was a truth so profound, it could not even be spoken or known. It had to be realized in the mind.

A mind that rests, even for a moment, is still. And in that stillness, there is an immaculate perfection. And in that perfection, there arises the lucidity to see things for how they are: how hard I am on myself, how internally competitive I have become, how judgmental and critical of things that I never ever find a moment's peace in my day. In such a mind, my head swells with morsels of panic, self-loathing, aggression, doubt, worry, and confusion until there is little room for anything else. I spent my life sorting this world into so many dualistic halves that I had become submerged under the accumulated soup of my opinions, judgments, and values swilling like flotsam in my mind.

This *feels* like who we are. We *identify* with these thoughts because, well, what else do we have to identify with? We have become used to the background noise in our heads. It is ubiquitous; our reference point for all that is *me* and *mine*.

But then, if we work diligently until our mind rests, even for a moment, and stillness awakens within, there arises a place so whole where none of that limiting judgment can survive. The tiny world of this and that, of right and wrong, of them and us, evaporates into paltry insignificance. Even if it is just for a second, we feel the ego annihilated and something...else... emerge into consciousness. And when we get there, we realize that we didn't get there because duality is a lie. We got there because *overcoming* the illusion of duality was *exactly* the process we needed. Only once we transcend the challenge facing every living creature can we see that the *process* was the purpose of the challenge. Those precious moments of life itself, from womb to grave, are the perfect tools by which liberty is attainable for us all.

Practicing non-judgment will be the hardest thing you have ever done, but it is supposed to be that way. It focuses the mind on the moment where consciousness grows and practical truth can unite with spiritual wisdom. The difficulty of this experiment in life is exemplified in all its glory by a global society that has totally lost its perspective on why we are here. We build cars for speed; we buy from the Internet for convenience; we work all day for income: our objectives have become utilitarian. We are focused on outcomes, not processes, and if we do focus on processes, we only do so for the utilitarian purpose of efficiency or productivity.

However, the human condition has forever been a search for meaning. That Zen koan built into the very architecture of the universe is not there to be solved. It is there to be surrendered to, for you to transform *during* the journey. When we focus on the process of *being human*, not on seeking the accomplishments of human beings, we will forever transform the yield of humanity. The material accomplishments of humankind are insignificant compared to the accomplishment of a single one of us being totally human.

Society can do this by uniting spiritual wisdom with practical truth. It is like uniting the two poles of electrical power, finding and mastering a process whereby daily judgments and profound non-judgment are used to create a third power: *consciousness*. It is not coincidental that these two poles are also known as *male* and *female*. Both literally and figuratively, the last 13,000 years have been a slow painful triumph of male energy over its female counterpart,[4] perfectly explaining how gender inequality and a whole host of other social inequalities have emerged.

Male energy is direct and forceful; female energy is indirect and subtle. As the post-Neolithic society began to value knowledge over feelings, logic over instinct, planning over spontaneity, force over subtlety, stoicism over sensitivity, and so forth, we lost touch with the power of the female mind. It is not a question of whether one type of energy is better than the other. Like water and rock, you need *both* to make a world. Consciousness is a product of unity, not division. It is found by uniting the two polarities, the two forces, the two powers into one. It is the skillful mastery of creation through the mental paradigm.

Sadly, from the Neolithic Revolution onwards, we geared up our world to legitimize the products of the unbalanced mind. The more it shaped our world, the more acceptable it became to perceive its imbalance as normal, and so the more we recreated it. Society was a perfect feedback loop for preexisting bias. It literally rewarded us, not for challenging it, but for reinforcing the status quo. Everything looked perfect, but that perfection was just our biases being reinforced by the reality we were creating.

In this environment, three things happened:

1. Female mental energy was suppressed by male mental energy
2. The male gender suppressed the female gender

3. Spiritual wisdom was dominated by practical truth.

The result was horrific trauma, exemplified by such atrocities as the witch-hunts of the mid-1400s to the mid-1700s, which took the lives of between 40,000 and 50,000 people,[5] up to 80% of whom were female.[6]

When the mind is unable to penetrate the illusion of practical truth and to balance useful judgments with the reality of no-self, we court social disaster. In contrast, a mind that can perceive practical truth as just that, *practical* but not exclusively *true*, is freed from its inherent constraints. Consciousness grows. And with it, the fruits of consciousness: compassion, empathy, and tolerance.

The metaphor of the child's journey from dualism into the adulthood of spiritual wisdom is perfect for this transformation. We are learning to *grow out* of the foolish mindset of absolutes and embrace the subtleties of spiritual wisdom. If we can scale back our dualistic mentality, the gradual process of maturing our judgmental little ego from the needy child into the discerning adult can begin. Dualism surely has its place in our world, but it is certainly not the way the world is.

However, from the Neolithic Revolution onwards, it was the way the world *seemed*. The cyclic Ages of Man revolved once more and practical truth would begin its long lumbering suppression of spiritual wisdom. With it, human consciousness stagnated. And while Golden Ages would flare up to remind us of our great potential, at work was a more profound power that would cast shade across time, across the collective culture, and eventually across the entire world. The ego-genie had been released from its bottle. And there wasn't a blind thing we could do to stop it.

Chapter 13

Enslavement by Stealth

You didn't choose to be an employee, did you? You didn't opt into the education system that conditions you, or the economic or political systems that fashion your life. And you certainly didn't choose to organize spiritual wisdom into religion, obscuring its profound purpose from us all. The march of time has molded a world in which we have entrusted our freedoms to proxies, to governments, corporations, and experts, and in doing so, those freedoms have been eroded to serve purposes that don't serve us.

Ego controls the world. All that took to happen was for ego to influence social purposes just 1% or 2% more each millennium than spiritual wisdom. A bit of greed here, a slight cruelty there, a dash of selfishness sprinkled on top; you wouldn't even notice. But after ten thousand years or more of this, it resulted in a wicked world indeed. We wouldn't even see it coming and, after it arrived, we wouldn't even know it was here. Most of us are too comfortable being uncomfortable to bother looking.

However, when we contextualize human history against the backdrop of impermanence and no-self shunned by ego, we see the difference between the progress we think we have made and the rut we are actually in. Only when we squint, look deeply, and gauge human progress against the spiritual metric of impermanence and no-self can we see how far we have fallen from the community, charity, and caring that once nurtured our humanity. These days, there's a new sheriff in town. And we're all obeying his law.

The dictionary describes a slave as being "a person who is the legal property of another and is forced to obey them." In the next two chapters, I want to discuss the concept of property and obedience as examples of spiritual, mental, and physical slavery. Through three powerful social examples, we will explore how history has brewed an increasingly coercive cocktail of culture in which individual power has been gradually relinquished to external forces we have trusted to control the world on our behalf. We will identify social systems and customs whose intentions appear benign but have been heavily influenced by ego's need to control and stratify. Indeed, we will learn how slavery is no historical blight confined to the recesses of our past, but endures today in both subtle and overt forms, exerting a stealthy hold on our collective psychology. Together, my three examples will tie the dawn of history to the roots of CLD, comprising an unholy trinity of systems that legitimize control and socialize the master/slave relationship.

We begin by answering the paradox that I posed at the end of Chapter 11. How could sedentary systems of agriculture ever be established and maintained when such a system is less efficient, less productive, and less healthy than nomadism? Farming is drudgery. It always has been, always will be, and it seems we'll do anything to make it easier on us. When they reached the continent of Africa in the fifteenth century CE, the hard reality of the agricultural life motivated the imperial Portuguese to begin kidnapping North Africans, thus initiating the infamous slave trade, which endured for over four centuries.

However, if you research slavery, you begin to realize that the master/slave relationship neither began nor ended during this period. Indeed, imperial slavery from the fifteenth to nineteenth century CE was no outlier in our global tale of inequity. It was entirely in character, the *continuation* of the social stratification that has been engineered since the dawn of history.

In his work *Cooperation and Its Evolution*, the Australian philosopher, Kim Sterelny, offers us a remarkable piece of the historical jigsaw. He identifies slavery as one of four coercive techniques responsible for supplanting egalitarian structures with social hierarchies after the Neolithic Revolution. Sterelny suggests that nomadic people would have never *willfully* abandoned their relatively cozy egalitarian lifestyle in favor of farming. Slavery was the only way this transformation made sense.

All the disadvantages of the agrarian lifestyle evaporate if you enslave people to do the spadework for you. So this is how the paradox of farming was overcome! What better way for one tribe to flourish than to attack another tribe, kill its men, and enslave its women? Indeed, this ugly possibility knits with our theory of how patriarchy became ubiquitous. Slavery of the female populace is exactly the kind of custom that, over the millennia, initiates deep-seated misogyny. After all, in the eyes of the male population, why would you treat the female gender equally when they are gaining a reputation for being of no greater value than a slave?

And so it began. From this moment in history forwards, slavery fashioned the world. Whether we are discussing Sumer, Greece, Egypt, Rome, and every dynasty since, slaves built them all. Indeed: "(in) the Roman Empire at the time of Augustus and later, the richest 5 percent of Italy's population owned one million house slaves (another two million were employed elsewhere, out of a total population of about 7.5 million people)."[1] That's the enslavement of 40% of the *entire* population!

We shouldn't imagine that this kind of hierarchical stratification was much different elsewhere. The fact is that slavery has always existed and it still does. It has a profound effect, not just on how a society of people relate to one another, but also on our expectations of what is fair and what is not. Shockingly, slavery is still a massive problem. Today, physical slavery is a bigger issue *than it has ever been*. Mauritania only officially abolished slavery in 2007, and 10–20% of the people in that Saharan nation are still estimated to be victims of it!

Indeed, according to Wikipedia, "The Global Slavery Index (2018) estimated that roughly 40.3 million individuals are currently caught in modern slavery, with 71% of those being female, and 1 in 4 being children."[2] In fact, there are *more people enslaved today than at any other point in human history.*

As the statistics show, humanity has little compunction about preying on the weak. It's been a common theme across antiquity and is still rife today. If you are reading this from a democratic, free, capitalist society, it may seem preposterous for me to propose that you too are enslaved in some way, but there are many ways and means to capture a human being. History bristles with examples of populations that assume they are too sophisticated to fall for the con. The Nazis, the Khmer Rouge, the Hutus of Rwanda: if entire nations of people can be convinced to participate in mass murder, how difficult do you think it would be to gently convince generation after generation of frogs all over the world to slowly lower themselves into a boiling pot?

Either subtly or overtly, through mental, physical, or spiritual means, over the ages we have been conditioned to accept the social structure of masters and servants in varying forms. Indeed, the human mind is ripe for it. All that is needed for people to give up our personal control is the projection of a fear and a White Knight that rides in to protect us from it. It is no less a lie that the powerful will protect and serve the interests of the weak than it is to read Lord Acton's saying about power and corruption and to believe that the powerful can stay good.

In modern times, the only factor that has changed is the *means* of your enslavement. In prehistory, we enslaved other local tribes. Then, we went international and enslaved people of other colors and continents. Next, we found a way to enslave the poor of our own nations with institutions like workhouses. And now, with physical slavery outlawed, the new, shinier, subtler version of this relationship is an employee under contract in a corporate power structure, now increasingly without a permanent contract or a union for support. Instead of the person being sold against their will, we are obliged to sell ourselves in a commercial environment called the labor market.

In the context of CLD, this marketplace seems a very reasonable arrangement. There appears to be a cosmos of difference between outright physical bondage and a contractual form of obligation. Surely that's a huge historical improvement? And I would not argue against that in principle. The difference between physical bondage and contractual obligation is vast to those affected by it, but *neither* of these conditions values the primacy of human spiritual needs, and that's the point.

All forms of bondage are concocted within the paradigm of practical truth. They do not come from the realm of spiritual wisdom because spiritual wisdom could no more chain a person than a knife repair a cut. Every form of social obligation we care to identify is carved from the linear tracks of the ego's response to the chaos of nature: control and hierarchy, and each is merely a subtle version of the next. These limitations are natural and unavoidable byproducts of ego in the same way that water makes things wet and heat makes things dry. They are the unambiguous fingerprints of our desire to impress our individual reality on the world, whether it wants it or not.

Unless we divorce our consciousness from this coercive culture entirely, we will be forever stuck in its closed loop. The duality of practical truth ensures it is an exclusive paradigm that denies the authenticity of the subjective reality beyond it. It preaches the Gospel of Personal Weakness, insisting that a hierarchy of elders, betters, or simply those who are wealthiest, must protect us through their benevolence because, for some unknown reason, we are not capable of doing this by ourselves. We're told that only those who are most successful in this world fit into this exclusive club of leaders but, not to worry, they want the best for us too. Yet, where do those of us outside this club really stand when none of those leaders talk of or practice the Three Marks of Existence, but in contrast build selfhood, control, and power in their own favor? What do we do when that same power has corrupted these echelons of control, and the coercion that is manufacturing social compliance is mixed into our social systems like a gin blended with tonic? It has taken us thousands of years to learn that it is the nature of the human ego to condition the weak to obey conventions that favor the strong and, in such a paradigm, the gap to freedom yawns wide. Indeed, it is as distant as the gap between practical truth and spiritual wisdom that we must all find a way to traverse if we are to make that leap to freedom.

Developing spiritual wisdom is not easy, but it is a sure way to value human industry differently than we currently do. The conventional ideology of the material economy cannot be reconciled with life's profound purpose. Freedom from suffering is not served by fueling materialism or desire in any way, shape, or form. The first step to liberty is for society to offer people an alternative: the spiritual wisdom of the Three Marks of Existence and the origins of defilements. On this foundation, free will begins to emerge. Suddenly, we have a real choice: do we pursue consciousness or not?

In our existing system, you have free will to choose your TV channel, your ice cream, and your pre-selected democratic candidates. But these choices are not significant. They are merely the fruits of our blind faith that we are in control. We so profoundly want to believe that our freedom is exemplified by having *more choices* that we are hypnotized into looking no deeper than the wonder of shelves stocked with 20 types of ketchup and factories mass-producing thousands of electronic devices. Yet, if each of those choices we are making culminates with us simply maintaining our ignorance of why we remain dissatisfied, then those choices are actually counterproductive to our freedom. They fool us into believing we are free, when the freedom we really have consists of little more than choosing whether we run around the big wheel, the small wheel, or the medium wheel. Regardless of the size of the wheel, we are each still just hamsters in a cage.

Apply the true scope of spiritual freedom to the average job and you will see how limited freedom really is. You have the free will to choose which company will pay you enough money to chase the multitude of ways you will pursue happiness, but this choice merely obliges you to labor for someone else's profit under an implicit economic threat: obey or face potential destitution. After all, can you really claim that your choice to sell your precious time to one organization or another is *real* physical freedom? It is Hobson's choice—take what is available or get nothing at all. That's not to say that all work is drudgery, but much of it is, and it will stay that way while society accepts the workplace as a means to an economic end rather than a process deeply connected to our spiritual progress and wellbeing.

In this regard, the principles of We-Topia offer us a real choice. Society can begin to reimagine the whole concept of human endeavor, our value, and what we do with our time here on Earth. Life is short. We get 80 years if we are lucky. We can structure a life path for the next generation in which business is not promoted as an opportunity to amass wealth but an opportunity to amass consciousness. Clearly, a society that teaches people the difference between chasing desires and chasing enlightenment empowers everyone to make the most valuable choice they will ever make: the pursuit of liberty or the acceptance of enslavement and ignorance. The point is not that we should be demanding one or the other or that society should be dogmatic about which it recommends. The point is that social systems can be designed to make clear what reality is and offer each of us an equal chance to choose a destiny of our own volition.

In such a culture, with such a purpose, it is inconceivable that we would replicate the existing systems of overproduction through contractual employment. This builds material freedom for a few wealthy individuals but spiritual captivity for the rest of us. We are so busy earning our salary, 40, 50, or 60 hours a week, that we have time for little else. The meat in this production sandwich, you and me, is but a utilitarian tool in a process of accumulation for owners.

The alternative is to break free from the paradigm of productivity and efficiency that pervades commercial enterprise and utilize a tribal model of experiential learning. This taps values such as teamwork, egalitarianism, and communal resources. Its purpose is not just production for profit but to develop a working environment in which the stakeholders' spiritual growth and development is valued and prioritized. In this way, the process of delivering goods or services is perceived as an opportunity to develop self-awareness. In the same way that a tribal life of hunting, cooking, or making clothes would have served the purpose of developing self-awareness in nomadic society, commercial productivity can do the same, if handled in a way that values the process over the outcome, and personal development over profit.

Trust and respect are key components in this system. It transforms the relationship between people in society and places the responsibility for building that trust on each of us. Once we are no longer competing for the best jobs, salaries, or positions, this becomes easier. We can shift the objectives of commerce from the volume and return on output to the quality and awareness generated during throughput. In such a commercial market, competition ebbs and cooperation grows because our contribution serves an optimized and honest environment of equal learning. Businesses no longer need to fight to be the market winner. Why would we even need hierarchical bosses and leaders in an enterprise where everyone is aligned in its purpose: you and me. Businesses that are founded upon the objective of realizing the Three Marks of Existence build enlightened people, first and foremost, as well as creating excellent products and services that the world needs to function and get better. Such a society is no longer a workforce of employees and owners. We are all workers *and* shareholders, owners *and* employees, producers *and* consumers. The purpose is no longer output. The process is the purpose. And in the very center of that process sit the most important thing on this Earth: *people*.

This objective offers commerce a very different perception of life and the tasks that we do. Whether washing dishes, making tools, or planning a sweeping global strategy, each has equal value when the process is purpose development. If we learn to value the present moment, each task, whatever it may be, offers equal opportunity for its curator to evolve consciousness. Happy, pressured, excited, afraid, or jealous, every moment is a chance to learn what your ego has become and how you can evolve with it. Working in such a business becomes a new experience—not about attaining endless goals and hitting more and more KPIs, but about enjoying a process that aspires to higher consciousness for each and every person involved in the moment.

It is also ironic that such an approach naturally improves productivity and efficiency. As trust builds between people, many innate inefficiencies in business control systems can be addressed. Ultimately, distrust is inefficient. So, building the deep-seated trust that can only exist between people who are in the job to make better people is an incredibly powerful and dramatic innovation. Not easy, of course, but possible when people are authentic and truly understand what the Three Marks of Existence mean. If we treat each commercial task as a new opportunity to see, feel, taste, smell, and hear, to experience the moment in which we can free ourselves from selfhood, so too do we free ourselves from the social trap of utilitarian jobs. This new vision of work offers a new social contract between commerce and people. It is an agreement of spirit, that the organization is fully invested in people's liberation from suffering and that the people are fully invested in the platform of opportunity the enterprise offers them to achieve that.

Modern employment is often a very shallow illusion of significance. Cognitive dissonance creates despair in a workforce obligated to perform menial tasks with little value to society that serve the basic purpose of accumulating private wealth for individuals. Whatever you want to call this situation, it is not liberty. But neither is it physical slavery. It is a subtle version of enslavement that falls somewhere in between the dualism of right and wrong. And that's how they get away with it.

We all sense this disconnect between our personal productivity and our essential spiritual needs. Society does not bridge the gap between professional and personal needs because it is not structured to meet the essential needs of people. Indeed, it does not even know what they are, or perhaps, care what they are. In reality, there is no such thing as a *professional*. This is just one more manipulative construct of words that only make sense to us because we have been conditioned to live in the reality where we need to work hard, ignore the suffering it might cause us, and sometimes even pretend that the products and services we create do not damage the world and its people as much as we suspect they do.

In truth, business is just people, doing, saying, learning, evolving, or not. Some of us thrive in that artificial creation called *the workplace* and others wilt because it jars with our very nature. If we lived in a society that understood the commonality between all human beings, we would be horrified that we are ignoring our higher spiritual needs in favor of something we call 'work.' But there is no such thing as work. It's all just life, lived consciously or not, and commerce can continue to be something we do while we wait for an opportunity to evolve, or it can actively participate in recreating itself in a form that truly understands human needs and what they must become to serve the evolution of our species.

It is an irony from the perspective of this chapter that the name Buddhadasa means 'Slave to the Buddha.' However, it illustrates something very important. Buddhadasa took this name because he intended to follow the Buddha's path wherever it took him. He did not have a professional life *and* a private life. It was one thing: life. And his life was his legacy. His intention was to dedicate himself to enlightenment. It is this concept of *intention* that defines who we are. Dedication to a pure idea, to spiritual wisdom, to attaining and sharing with others a higher truth, is the kind of slavery that makes a mockery of dualism, for the culmination of this slavery is freedom from suffering.

This is how the world revolts. This is sedition in its purest of forms, for it eschews the values of a confused and angry world and turns one's own life into a testimony to the power of peaceful effort and action. In contrast, slavery to ignorance of our worth, to suppress our personal power, and to limit our spiritual potential, manifests all of society's ills. We don't know how to express this frustration peacefully or manage the emotion that it awakens within us. Our diet of desires and attachments feeds the illusion that we can improve the feeling inside by changing the world outside. All this does is cede our power to more illusions, buying into the lure of materialism at the cost of spiritual wisdom. For some, these illusions still end in physical slavery. For others, it is a contract, a low-paid job, and the threat of bills. But for us all, wherever we may be and however high up the hierarchical ladder we may go, being entrained in the pursuit of unsatisfactoriness is slavery in all but name.

Chapter 14

Law and Money

The statistics on modern slavery demonstrate that the world is still gripped by its physical blight. But what these statistics don't show is the mental and spiritual tentacles that enslave us in more subtle ways. Indeed, the social systems of CLD are the sophisticated heir of outright physical bondage. They support and legitimize the relationship between the controlled and the controller through subtle means.

This is perfectly exemplified by Sterelny's second coercive trigger: the *threat of exclusion from the community*. In modern parlance, this is known as *the criminal justice system*. As Sterelny predicts it would be, this system is so bursting with threats and controls that if you fall foul of its rules, some governments might legally be required to murder you! You can't get any more enslaved than dead! It really ties you down.

Joking aside, I am not arguing that criminal law is not useful in principle. It is like the problem of duality. It has a place, but it should never be applied without a firm foundation of values in place. For example, if we are all equal under the law, how is it that wealth and influence make a mockery of this principle? It is no secret that money buys better lawyers, wins more political influence, and settles out-of-court cases that would convict a poorer man to prison.

As this simple example demonstrates, the legal system has its problems, but this is just the tip of the iceberg. The true outrage of the legal system is hidden in proprietary law. As the old Scottish expression goes: "Possession is eleven points in the law, and they say there are but twelve," which gives us the more common saying: "Possession is nine-tenths of the law."

By axiom at least, the primary purpose of the legal system is not criminal jurisprudence, but to manage *who has what*.

Effectively, proprietary law is social and economic inertia by decree. It protects the hierarchical status quo by assuring an owner's continuing right to possession. The irony will not be lost on the reader that the first example of law ever found, the Code of Hammurabi, a legal text from Babylonia dating to circa 1755–1750BCE, contained multiple statutes governing *slave ownership*, rights, and punishments. This is no mere coincidence. In modern times, property law has enshrined these rights. If one family acquired a piece of land a thousand years ago, regardless of how they acquired it or whether they utilize it today, the law gives them the right to retain it. Indeed, there is a whole judicial system in place to prevent desperate people from using that land and to oust them from it if they dare to do so.

In contrast, there is no law in place that permits the destitute to use what the wealthy do not use. And yet, which of these is more moral? My point is that the notion of law as a moral code is sketchy, to say the least. On the contrary, the foremost articles of law enshrine the right of the powerful to continue to dominate and control. Wealth and property are materialized power, and property law is simply a stealthy vehicle for the retention of that power. When we peel back the rationale that proprietary law exists solely to bring order to possessions, we see the sticky fingerprints of ego all over it. It is the ego's Holy Grail to live forever and while it cannot (yet) do that, the next best thing is the hereditary transfer of the possessions that represent a person's life.

The legacy of this ambition is a map of the world that supports societal inertia. Look around! The Lurie family of Israel can be traced back to 1037BCE! The Imperial House of Japan was founded in 660BCE! The Kong family of China has its roots in 551BCE! And, of course, that most venerated of all institutions, the British Royal Family, can be traced back to 993CE! I don't name these families to shame them or to suggest they are the bad guys in this story just because they are wealthy. My purpose in this book is to empower individuals, but to do that we must be absolutely certain of how we have been disempowered. Yes, it is rational that those people who own something should keep it. But is it moral when, for example, "432 families own half the private lands in Scotland, and just over 1200 landowners hold 2/3 of Scotland's lands."[1] This is not just or moral. It is inertia.

Both physical bondage and the centralization of resources create servitude. While physical bondage is its most visceral version, the law threatens punitive action to monopolize resources and maintain social inertia. Both also have their origins in the Neolithic Revolution. However, there is a third kind of servitude that I like to think of as a kind of spiritual enslavement, because it most effectively captivated our egos and turned the world into a competition of power: *money*.

The invention of money was also directly related to agriculture. It resulted due to a phenomenon unique to sedentary communities: *overproduction*. Nomadic tribes simply took what they needed and moved on, but as sedentary communities became established, surplus production was possible. It was either consumed, given away, or left behind.

But sedentary villages grew. They interacted with other settled tribes in their locality and, for the first time in history, trustworthiness became a problem. Due to the "double coincidence of wants,"[2] barter was impractical. Crops didn't necessarily ripen at the same time, so trust had to rule this system. If I gave you apples today and you had nothing to trade, I had to trust you that you'd help me out when I came back later. However, as villages grew, tribal families became aggregates of many families, and neighboring villages no longer knew each other with the same level of trust.

As we have noted, the notion of trusting strangers does not sit easily in the human mind, and so a system that relied upon trust was fertile ground for invention. What was needed was a middleman, a system that bridged the problem of the double coincidence of wants and the gradual erosion of trust between communities.

Money was that system. Economists and sociologists alike laud the development of currency as a form of account. It was a watershed in human history that transformed a transaction of personal trust into an impersonal system that guaranteed equal value in the future. From this foundation, trade flourished, prosperity grew across the world, and civilization began. Suddenly, the value of a crop need never again be lost through spoilage. Everything had a value. It seemed like the perfect system by which the humble farmer's return on investment of time and effort was guaranteed...

Or so they say. But beneath the conventional theory of money there lurks a far darker interior.

Firstly, let's not forget that the humble farmer in our story was probably a slave of a powerful landowner. So, the only return on her investment that she was going to get was less of a beating if her endeavors returned a surplus! And secondly, why would a close-knit egalitarian society feel the need to hoard value? The simple answer is that it didn't. At least, not until *distrust* set in. As communities swelled in number and the close-knit bonds of nomadic tribes began to erode, villages of dozens, then hundreds, then communities of thousands of people fragmented the bonds of trust that had once united nomadic tribes. Trade with other communities refocused the efforts of a village from building community, to building status and hierarchical power. As implicit trust was superseded by an explicit token of value, history stood at a momentous crossroads. We had manufactured a symbol of unprecedented allure. It had such enormous potential that through its creation the higher calling of the human spirit could be eradicated and be replaced by a proxy for ego. Money not only changed the world forever.

It also forever perverted the direction of travel of the human spirit and, with it, human evolution.

Money is the biggest IOU ever written. It started as notches carved into the bones of animals, predating writing by some considerable time. It eventually evolved into tokens of currency, a universal form of credit that gradually displaced one's honor, one's word, one's honesty, and one's memory, to represent everything the new world stood for—a reality of overproduction where implied value could be hoarded forever in symbolic tokens.

This was not just a material revolution. It was a *spiritual* calamity. An invisible, intangible, experiential God was unseated as the ultimate power in the universe and a new reign began: a material token of wealth that could be touched, counted, and hoarded. If anything in the world represents the difference between spiritual wisdom and material truth, it is that image. Trust in the community was then free to erode, because your personal word was less valuable than the weight of your impersonal stash. Wealth equaled status, and status equaled direct control over your world. In this new paradigm, spiritual notions of personal power and freedom from attachment were perverted into material concepts of hoarding value and using it to buy companionship, loyalty, land, influence, and your heart's desire. Our planet was no longer being run by the people who were the most respected and loved in the village, but by the people with the most tokens.

The true impact of money was a spiritual shift towards a reliance on 'me' rather than 'us.' When I have money, I don't have to trust anyone to feed me. I don't have to trust anyone to shelter me. I don't have to trust anyone to clothe me. My survival does not rely upon a community to share what they have. I can do this alone. I only need *me* and *mine* to hoard the value of other people's production. That's not only a massive motivation to become selfish; it also drives the culture of coercion that disempowers the populace while individuals harness the wealth generated from their labor. The true effect of money is like a comet landing smack-bang in the middle of our species' spiritual diorama. It obliterated the three-dimensional shape of the world and left our entire species nursing a deep spiritual scar.

Money is a transparent extension of the masculine mind. It is a material form of power and control that hands the spiritual destiny of society to the hoarding mentality of our wealthiest members. This is cemented by varying degrees of physical slavery, legitimized by legal statutes, and symbolized by tokens that supplant the higher pursuit of spiritual liberty with material wealth. Overproduction quickly became the most popular game in town. Not only was it the fastest and most reliable means for those with the most goods to acquire the most power and control; it also accelerated every ecological problem that we are experiencing in the twenty-first century.

Is this mere hyperbole? A little ideological hubris, perhaps? Well, consider it. The tragic result of money is a world where spiritual purpose has been corrupted. Meanwhile the planet is punch-drunk and staggering from the consequences of overproduction and the resulting ecological trauma. Our economy is a race to transmute real and finite natural resources to feed our infinite desire for endless 'me' and 'mine.' Just weigh up all this absurdity against a reality of no-self and ask if it is hyperbole to suggest that we are deluded by a fantasy. We have transformed something natural and real into products of no intrinsic value, exchanging them for a worthless token, assigned with a fake power, that serves the objectives of an illusory ego and its lust for a false identity. At its most fundamental level, we have become slaves to a token worth nothing, serving something that does not exist. This is delusion in a nutshell.

Across history this same trend is repeated: individual ego hijacks society for personal gain, again and again, and again. It is a pattern carved deeply into the face of the twenty-first century. CLD's legacy is the primacy of personal choice. Its weapons of economic supremacy are corporate entities and perpetual international conflict over resources and power. The truth, sadly, is that the social systems shaping our world are the schemes of people who have lost their connection to spiritual wisdom and rely upon the dichotomies of practical truth. They seek personal control by monopolizing the fruits of other people's overproduction, making unjust laws that legitimize their continued right to prosper and hoard. And money, their acquired power, is but a means to control their destiny at the expense of those who labor on their behalf.

As Tolstoy put it most eloquently: "Money is a new form of slavery, and distinguishable from the old simply by the fact that it is impersonal—that there is no human relation between master and slave." Exchange the word 'money' in Tolstoy's statement with 'corporatization' or 'social hierarchy' or 'law' and the principle from his message remains broadly true. The great illusion at work is that democracy and money are freedoms demonstrating our social liberty when they actually disguise our bondage in clever ways. We have all been indoctrinated to believe that the systems of labor, law, and currency we currently have are the *only* ways that a reasonable society can be run. But the truth is that we have sleepwalked into a physical, mental, and spiritual master/slave relationship over the course of 13,000 years.

This isn't *the* reality. It is just *a* reality that has become comfortable to the majority of us while we seek pleasure through unsatisfactoriness! In this artificial construct, the natural world order has been turned on its head. Up has become down, down has become up, and the notion of egalitarian inclusivity has been relegated to the reverie of mad idealists like me.

With the conventions of employment, property law, and currency firmly ensconced, the restructuring of society from egalitarian interdependence to hierarchical domination was complete. This is *the* way, so we are told. This is the *best* we can do, so we have learned. This is *progress*, so we believe. Meanwhile, a wealthy posse of masculine minds possesses the labor and energy of the majority through stealth. Their system of labor strives for sanitized inequality. Their system of economy buys sanitized inequity. And their system of law enforces sanitized inertia. In this system, those who have the power maintain their possession of it. *Forever*.

So, that's it, right? We're victims. The world will forever be owned and carved up into personal property and the little guy will be forever a victim of that? Well, no. That's not it at all. The thing about earthly power is that it is all an illusion. When you stop and consider what you can personally control, you realize that control through possession is like mist. Yes, you can see it, but you cannot really hold it. One day, you will be gone. Then, what will you hold? The sleight of hand our globalized system practices is nothing more than the techniques mastered by the world's finest illusionists. They train the eyes of the population on a glittering prize worth nothing, while they hide away life's true treasures behind a curtain.

What lies behind that curtain is your spirit. Every system we have discussed in this book so far is like a psy-op, exclusively inculcating you into a practical truth that rarely serves your higher purpose. The architecture of society limits your personal spiritual potential through an intense focus on physical manifestation. Inertia requires that this powerful influence remains in place. Indeed, the greatest fear of those who have control is that you will realize how immensely powerful you are, with or without physical freedom. For thousands of years, our personal power has been hidden away from us, and the global order relies upon you remaining unconscious. But somebody, somewhere in this world, knows what you have forgotten, and it scares the living daylights out of them that, one day, you might remember what it is they took and see who took it from you for what they really are.

Chapter 15

We-Topia: You Have Control

Let me tell you a story.

Once upon a time, we were all savages. We lived as nomads in a hand-to-mouth existence. We subsisted in a threatening, fear-filled world in which we organized ourselves into a lawless and cruel society that promoted a dog-eat-dog, survival-of-the-fittest competition.

And then, after a short, miserable life, we died.

However, one day, all that changed. Agriculture blossomed and civilization soared. We united in villages, initiated stronger social structures, specialized in new skills, improved technologies, and built powerful inter-community trading systems. From this moment forwards, the world of today was shaped by progress, civilization, and a freer, fairer society where the cruelty of nomadism could be forever relegated to history...

Oh, and there were probably rainbows and pixies in their somewhere too.

This, say the historians and economists of today, is the true story of humankind. And they're sticking to it.

The problem with this little tale is that *it never occurred*. It is a myth; a fable of progress reflecting the psychological need of today's people to believe that we are somehow *better* and *more advanced* than the savages who preceded us. Of course we do! It's a natural inclination. After all, it is estimated that 100 billion people[1] have lived on the planet over the last 13,000 years or so. If this multitude of lives was not spent in the pursuit of some higher glory but merely served as chattel in a slow deterioration of morality, well, what does that say about the world that you and me live in today?

What does it say, indeed?

The true legacy of farming, law, money, trade, and so on, is no fairy tale with a happy ending. Conventional history may weave a merry yarn from the hand-to-mouth existence of nomadism to the utopia of supermarket aisles full of processed goods, but be warned: historians go to great lengths to paint our species' journey as a long trek through the woods of a gloomy past to a house made of candy in a bright colorful future. But they all omit the part where, inside the house, the wolf waits to gobble us up.

If progress is nothing more than a technological foot-race from flint to Teflon and arrows to smart bombs then, my goodness, there's no doubt that humanity has already cracked the God-code and advanced at the speed of a satellite orbiting the planet. But when we place all that progress against the yardstick of humanity's spiritual development, a path whose success is determined by how effective we are at eliminating defilements, our story arc bends towards calamity and ends up in a land far, far away from a happy ending.

Slavery has many forms. Its most ubiquitous is not the chains that deprive a person of their physical liberty but the mental constraints that blind us to how faithfully we have been serving the illusion of 'me' and 'mine.' This is the truest representation of the human story. Were it victimless, we might call it a comedy. If its history were not well documented, it could be a fantasy. But, as I have shown in this book, it is actually a slow-burning entrapment within systems that value independence over interdependence, personal power over group wellbeing, and competitive social attitudes over cooperation. And that is a tragedy.

Coercion triggered the Neolithic Revolution in some temperate glade of the Fertile Crescent in the Middle East, and its effects still pervade the world today. The difference is that this coercion is no longer local and tribal. Computers, mobile technologies, and the Internet render no mind beyond the reach of its omnipresent tentacles. The coercers have become so skilled at manipulating human psychology that even the prospect of endless, consistent defeat has been embraced by the majority, the quiet, passive losers in this tale of time.

In the words of Buddhadasa:

Time is running out. In our adhammic quests we are destroying one another. We are denying what it means to be a human being within nature, namely, mutuality, give-and-take and the building of the sort of system that will prevent both destruction and the divisions that deny the mutually co-arising nature of our world. We have created the most demeritorious age of humankind, one which attempts to defy the laws of nature...It is imperative that we cultivate those higher qualities of mind and spirit that we, as humans, have within us. We must not allow ourselves to lose our humanity...We must realize that the foundation of real socialism is Dhamma, Nature (dhammajati), the laws of Nature, the truth of Nature (dhammasacca).[2]

Just because you and I are not held against our will in physical bondage, it doesn't mean we are not enslaved. It reminds me of a quote by Mark Twain: "How easy it is to make people believe a lie, and how hard it is to undo that work again!" My intention in writing We-Topia is not to change the world. It is to impress upon you how effortlessly we can be deceived and how easily that candle of light inside you can be dimmed to a flicker without you even knowing. Rather than using that flame to burn through the illusions of ego and illuminate the whole universe with no-self, we have been taught to use it to fuel personal identity on a quest for permanence and status. To this end, we have welcomed into our homes a Patriot Act-inspired, shelter-in-place ordered, stop-and-search controlled, video and online surveilled reality stripped bare of the freedoms our ancestors took for granted. And we believe this makes us *freer*. But how can we ever be freer through embracing more control?

I believe that, as we embrace more security, we sacrifice part of what it means to be human. Buddhadasa warned us against abandoning our humanity, but what does it really mean to be human? I believe that our highest humanity is characterized by a potential to realize spiritual wisdom in a uniquely powerful way. It is this unrivaled quality that inspired arahants and Golden Ages on the Earth. And it is this quality that is the true meaning of We-Topia: the personal potential within you to attain absolute freedom from desire and attachment. If we continue down a path of endless pursuit of selfhood, that place of refuge within us, that little We-Topia of the mind, will remain forever hidden from us all, and with it, the potential of our entire species.

Ultimately, this is the unfulfilled power to effect global change that we each possess. It is no illusion. It is no hyperbole. Indeed, it is a truth so powerful and so frightening to those who hold all the material wealth and status at this time, that they have hidden it from us all for millennia. But to set forth on this journey of realization with big plans of global upheaval, revolution, ideological reform, or political conflict, would be a big mistake. We will surely fail. Just as spirituality was organized and corrupted thousands of years ago, every spiritual movement has been corrupted since, because that is what organization does: it corrupts. Moreover, if you hand me that power, or someone else in a movement, or another group of people, you place your hopes and ambitions in proxies who, I'm sorry to say, can never and will never create We-Topia for you.

We-Topia is *personal* transformation. It is a mindset that provides you with a refuge to experience the world in peace and through a filter of calm. This movement is not about large groups of people demanding change, but about what happens in your own home where your power to be whatever you want to be is unassailable. Such a force of change is an unstoppable revolution. The power of each of us to transform, quietly, with zero fanfare and with no additional resources, status, or influence at all, is the ultimate sedition. It is the inexorable force meeting the immovable object, resulting in the most profound of hushed explosions, in the most silent of ways, that no video surveillance or phone tap will ever hear. The next revolution will *not* be televised.

The power of personal transformation is the secret of humanity that has been perverted and obscured over the ages, for were this purpose ever to be taken seriously by the population of the planet, society would collapse and a new Earth would begin. In such an event, there would be no stopping the evolution of our species or the natural, gentle adaptation of the global community. Everything that is wasteful, or harmful or addictive, or confusing, would stop simply because the people of the world had stopped being distracted from the moment and become focused on the impermanence of all things, where the output of our hearts and minds creates the changing world.

However, our ambition should not be a utopian fantasy. We must be focused on what we can do, now. I realize that few people are ready for the effort of change, and so we must each pick up our obligations one by one, on our own terms, at our own time. This means that We-Topia is the realization and acceptance of three simple words: *you have control*. You already know the Three Marks of Existence. You already know the cause of defilements. You choose what you do with that information: something or nothing? What happens next is up to you. No one, regardless of their wealth, power, or influence, can stop you from *being* what you want to be, for that is the choice you make at every moment of your day. On the bus, in a crowd, at a party, during a walk, after a coffee, over a weekend, during a struggle, after a day at work: no one, at any time or place, can prevent your awareness expanding along the path of liberty. Spirituality is about who you are, and life is a simple sum: your personal potential realized. Or not. You are now free to choose the future of your own freedom.

Will you continue to be at war with the world as the world trains its guns on you? Will you continue to fabricate competition as society says you must? Will you play the social roles that ask you to hate and criticize, as so many of us do? Or will you step away, stop watching, refuse to buy in, ignore it, walk out from it, and leap into a new world with a new ambition: total personal liberty? You have been lied to, or at the very least, dispossessed of your birthright, and it is time for you to choose whether you keep participating in ignorance, or wake up to awareness.

No, it's not easy. It is work: diligent work. But a single day of hard work towards freedom is worth a thousand days of comfort in slavery. Buddhadasa's dream of social unity was not some hippie-style cult or a love-in utopian fantasy. It was a hard fact, waiting at the end of a real choice: work to be at one with your own nature and take back control of your liberty — or not.

When I was quite young I used to wake up at night, draw back the curtains of my room, and stare up at the stars. I felt that something had gone terribly wrong with the world. I would look out at the cloudless sky, pricks of light peppering the dark shawl above my head, and I felt the outrageous volume of reality bearing down on me. I was but a crumb in that expanse and, in the enormous significance of everything around me, I found my comfort.

It was at those moments that I sensed the profound and divine magic everywhere. It wasn't mine. I was merely floating in it, borrowing it. Yet I was confused because I saw that people everywhere were busy taking the credit for the things they conjured up from this magic. They perceived themselves as the source of the ocean when I saw each of us as a mere molecule blessed with the power of the entire sea. Their illusion of power came from possessing what they could never own and holding on to what cannot be grasped. In my head, the whole world was upside down. Why did no one seem to care or notice how many of us were slipping and falling off its surface?

I later came to know that many people feel the way I felt. Intuitively, we all sense that we are borrowing this identity. We know on one level that we are the temporary creators of a shape and form. Just as Earth is a vehicle around the sun, the body is a vehicle for consciousness upon the Earth, and every human being walks a personal quest for liberty from the illusions of permanence and selfhood.

This feeling I felt as a child, this vague sensation of displacement, was my spirit urging me to address the direction of travel that my life would take thereafter. Would I use that sensation of unease to slip quietly into the physical world where I would have plenty of company? Or would I use it for the lonely journey to the furthest reaches of the spiritual world, where a different community entirely awaited my choice?

Maybe you have felt that way too. Maybe you still do. Or maybe, one morning soon, perhaps tomorrow, or next month or maybe five years from now, you will wake up with the same unease in your head. This is no fault of your brain or your body chemistry. Don't take a pill for it. It is simply time. It may be just a minor thought running like a broken record through your mind, or a vivid explosive crisis uprooting your life, but you will know that something is inherently wrong. As you lie there in your bed, or drive your car to work, or play with your children, or walk the dog, you too may feel the burden of society on your shoulders, the well of anger and frustration stored in the billions of minds trapped in a reality that doesn't make sense. The full mass of global inertia will bear down upon your body like an ongoing crash into something unbearable, the entire volume of Earth's history momentarily like an anvil on your chest, as the concertinaing of each evolution in technology and social systems plows into the present moment of your life.

At that moment it might seem like the chaos of the material world is far too much to bear, but you will realize that such a feeling has been there all your life, humming away in the background of your thoughts. And this time, on this day, at this moment, the sheer scale of all that weight will not intimidate you. You will no longer use it to justify your choice to stay pinned beneath its hulking shapes and forms. You will accept that, yes, it will be harder to move when you are so encumbered by a history that requires your mindless silence and your motionless acquiescence. But on this day, at that hour, you will finally decide that *you have control of everything that needs controlling*. Powerlessness is the illusion evoked by the myth of material power, but once you *choose* to move, once you *choose* to free yourself from the path of materialism and permanence, inertia will shift to your side. The hard yards are done. Your journey towards We-Topia will be impossible to stop.

Control can be imposed upon you from outside, but there is no scenario in which freedom can be externally imposed upon you. You must do that yourself. We-Topia is a sacred place cultivated in the mind. It begins with realizing the natural interdependence of all things, and ends in the reality of impermanence and no-self. That is why spiritual communities were created in the past and that is why they will be created in the future. But we must start from humble origins again, from within, before finding ways to support connections between like-minded people within the spiritual community that already exists all over the world. We are not separate or alone but intimately connected by the forces that bind all things together as one. With effort, we can influence our self to see the prevailing illusions we have all believed in. But we cannot choose on behalf of someone else to break free from those illusions, nor can we do the work for them once they have made the choice. We-Topia is a place of personal transformation because the only revolution that makes a difference is your own, chosen by you, worked by you, and followed through to the end by you.

Each of us, at the end of our own story, will be measured not by how many scrapes we avoided, but how many dark and dangerous places we entered, unsure of where we were headed next. I know it is scary. I know it is difficult. But so is the illusion we have snuggled up against all our lives. In a way, if ego split society into strata and filled it with tiny egos at war with each other, We-Topia is a dream that connects these splintered spirits back together again, person by person. It rejoins each of us to a lineage of struggle, to the kindred spirits across all of history, until we all make an unbroken chain, unified in every way.

Everything is interdependent, even time and especially spirit. We-Topia draws from that infinite ocean of energy that inspired Golden Ages past and bore arahants on the wings of liberty. The physical presence of these days and characters may be lost to our eyes, but nothing ever disappears from the ether. It's all impermanent. It's all no-self. But even that leaves an imprint, a record of our struggle to exist in different shapes and forms carved into the architecture of the universe.

Is We-Topia a dream? There's no harm in dreaming. Nomads lived in dreams. Modern people live in dreams too. The difference is that, to maintain our current reality, everyone must embrace an illusion together, but to dream of We-Topia we must wake up separately, one person at a time. Then we can join together. But if we believe we must change the world to make a difference, we will never take the first step forwards. Evolution will stall for another 13,000 years while we wait for the odds of success to shift from impossible to absolutely certain. The path to your enlightenment is inevitable, but it only becomes inevitable when you say it is.

We-Topia is already yours. It is a state of sentience bequeathed to you by gift economies, personified by ancient masters, written into the texts of the enlightened, and perfected by the arahants who have borne the torch of spiritual evolution across the desert of time. Through We-Topia, our spirits brighten the world. "Work diligently," Buddha said, for burning inside you is a source of greater power and abundance than you have ever imagined possible. It is not limited by the bonds of physicality or divided by the duality of the mind. It is a single, small flame that, like the arahants who came before you, will illuminate the entire universe as you learn to illuminate yourself.

Author's Note

We-Topia is about action. All of us need a little help with this, so to help you build momentum after reading this book, I have produced a few practical We-Topia guides. These are designed to help you build a personal set of mindfulness habits, connect with like-minded people in your community, and establish how We-Topia could be extended out into the wider world where millions of people are waiting for support and the chance to grow in ways that have been hidden from them all their lives.

Each of these guides is available for *free for download* from my website www.michaelpaulstephens.com

They are:

- We-Topia Guide One: A Practical Guide to Meditation that Really Works
- We-Topia Guide Two: A Guide to Share Circles
- We-Topia Guide Three: A Guide to the Six Principles of We-Topia

We-Topia begins with you, but it doesn't end with you. It can build. It can grow. We can create communities that, at their heart, care about who we are and why we are here. It's been done before. The only thing stopping us is effort. Everything else, we already have.

Previous Titles

Provolution
A Guide to Changing the World
Through Personal Evolution
Available from O-Books and online retailers

You are the only thing in the world you can change. And when you change, the whole world changes with you.

Provolution invites you on an odyssey of personal transformation from your mind, your body and your spirit, guiding you towards the natural wellbeing, emotional freedom and spiritual peace you deserve. From endemic global egotism to the enduring deception of time, *Provolution* describes how the world has become stuck in a spiral of suffering perpetuated by flawed ideas that have endured for millennia.

Drawing upon natural concepts like human spirit, uni-time, i-go, and relational mirrors, *Provolution* empowers you with real-world skills to take back control of a future that you have relinquished to an illusion of fear and to transcend the conditioning that compels you to suffer. *Provolution* is your guide to spiritual evolution in a world that likes your suffering exactly as it is. If you're seeking global change, begin by provolving your own.

Equanimous
A Channeled Dialog of The Past, Present and
Future of Humanity
Available for download from www.michaelpaulstephens.com

In 2010, Michael was busy jotting down notes about "the reset." To him, it was already remarkable information received from his channeled guide, Master Jacob.

But today, over a decade later, it is even more remarkable. Now, in the age of COVID, everyone is talking about the "Great Reset."

Written by Michael Paul Stephens and channeled by his wife, Orranut, *Equanimous* is a gripping conversation between Michael and his spirit guide, Master Jacob.

It recounts the awe-inspiring story of how the universe really began and the secret evolution of humanity, and offers dramatic revelations about the lives of Buddha and Jesus Christ. The fast-paced dialog of *Equanimous* delivers astonishing revelations on every page.

Revealing the true origins of humanity's past, our present, and the future, it is the remarkable insight to The Reset that is most startling. Master Jacob takes you through what is happening with COVID today, what will be happening soon and why.

Equanimous is more than just a spiritual book. It is the book of our times. It asks us all to leave behind the old interpretations of God, the universe and our life's purpose and to wake up to The Reset: a future where the world will be reborn.

The challenge for each human being is simple: Do you dare to have no fear?

Why On Earth Are You Here?
A Guide to Your Life's Spiritual Purpose on Earth
Available for download from www.michaelpaulstephens.com

What is the meaning of life? Why was I born? Does consciousness have a purpose? In this remarkable book, Michael Paul Stephens answers every question you may have on life's meaning and purpose. He explains the universe in ways that are novel, inspiring and groundbreaking for a whole new generation of spiritual seekers.

Unfulfilled by religious doctrine and uninspired by new age terminology, *Why on Earth Are You Here?* captures the imagination of a new audience ready to explore their spiritual potential. It offers a profound insight into the spiritual implications of physics, bringing meaning to your life and explaining why the reality of the world we have created is so unfulfilling for so many of us.

The universe comes alive, not as a mechanical instrument of physics but as a living, conscious entity that encapsulates, within every atom and molecule, a profound message of hope for us all. This message, carried through from the subatomic world to the formation of planets, and from the evolution of life to the creation of individual consciousness, will help you reanimate your world, bring meaning and purpose to life and answer the deeper questions of *Why on Earth Are You Here?*

Notes

Introduction
1. Buddha-Dhamma can be translated as 'the teachings of the Buddha.'

Chapter 1: The Purest Natural Socialism
1. Buddhadasa Bhikkhu. Dhammic Socialism. p110. Thai Inter-Religious Commission for Development, Bangkok. 1993 (2nd edition). Translated by Donald K. Swearer.
2. Ibid. pp117–118.
3. Ibid. p118.

Chapter 2: A Society of Winners and Losers
1. Tanzi, A., Dorning, M. Top 1% of U.S. Earners Now Hold More Wealth Than All of the Middle Class. October 8, 2021. Bloomberg. [Internet]. [Cited January 31, 2022]. Available from: https://www.bloomberg.com/news/articles/2021-10-08/top-1-earners-hold-more-wealth-than-the-u-s-middle-class#:~:text=The%20top%201%25%20represents%20about,the%20country's%20major%20political%20battles.
2. Ibid.
3. Schaeffer, K. 6 facts about economic inequality in the U.S. February 7, 2020. Pew Research Center. [Internet]. [Cited January 31, 2022]. Available from: https://www.pewresearch.org/fact-tank/2020/02/07/6-facts-about-economic-inequality-in-the-u-s/.
4. State of Homelessness: 2021 Edition. National Alliance to End Homelessness. [Internet]. [Cited January 31, 2022]. Available from: https://endhomelessness.org/homelessness-in-america/homelessness-statistics/state-of-homelessness-2021/#:~:text=The%20Basics,Special%20Populations.

5. Strauss, V. Hiding in plain sight: The adult literacy crisis. November 1, 2016. The Washington Post. [Internet]. [Cited January 31, 2022]. Available from: https://www.washingtonpost.com/news/answer-sheet/wp/2016/11/01/hiding-in-plain-sight-the-adult-literacy-crisis/?noredirect=on.

6. Prescription Drugs. Georgetown University; Health Policy Institute. [Internet]. [Cited January 31, 2022]. Available from: https://hpi.georgetown.edu/rxdrugs/.

7. Terlizzi, E.P., Zablotsky, B. Mental Health Treatment Among Adults: United States, 2019. NCHS Data Brief No. 380. September 2020. Centers for Disease Control and Prevention. [Internet]. [Cited October 10, 2021]. Available from: https://www.cdc.gov/nchs/products/databriefs/db380.htm.

8. Schaeffer, K. 6 facts about economic inequality in the U.S. February 7, 2020. Pew Research Center. [Internet]. [Cited March 25, 2022]. Available from: https://www.pewresearch.org/fact-tank/2020/02/07/6-facts-about-economic-inequality-in-the-u-s/.

9. De Vos, J.M., Joppa, L.N., Gittleman, J.L., Stephens, P.R., Pimm, S.L. Estimating the normal background rate of species extinction. Conservation Biology. Volume 29, Issue 2, April 2015, pp452–462. Society for Conservation Biology. [Internet]. [Cited March 25, 2022]. Available from: https://conbio.onlinelibrary.wiley.com/doi/abs/10.1111/cobi.12380.

10. Thornhill, T. WWF Living Planet Report Warns That By 2030 Two Earths Will Be Needed To Sustain Our Lifestyles. May 16, 2012. Huffington Post. [Internet]. [Cited March 25, 2022]. Available from: https://www.huffingtonpost.co.uk/2012/05/16/wwf-warns-that-we-will-need-two-earths-by-2030_n_1520449.html#:~:text=ParentsClimate%20Crisis-,WWF%20

Living%20Planet%20Report%20Warns%20That%20By%20
2030%20Two%20Earths,Needed%20To%20Sustain%20
Our%20Lifestyles&text=Humans%20will%20need%20
two%20Earths,a%20new%20report%20has%20warned.
11. Smith, A. An Inquiry into the Nature and Causes of the
Wealth of Nations. Book V, Chapter I, Part II: Of the Expense
of Justice. March 17, 2001 [eBook #3300]. [Internet]. [Cited
March 25, 2022]. Available from: https://www.gutenberg.
org/files/3300/3300-h/3300-h.htm.

Chapter 3: The Purpose of Life

1. Buddhadasa Bhikkhu. Dhammic Socialism. p75. Thai Inter-
Religious Commission for Development, Bangkok. 1993
(2nd edition). Translated by Donald K. Swearer.

Chapter 4: Evolution of Mind

1. Hampton, D. How Your Thoughts Change Your Brain,
Cells and Genes. March 23, 2016. Updated March 24, 2017.
[Internet]. [Cited December 18, 2021]. Available from:
https://www.huffpost.com/entry/how-your-thoughts-
change-your-brain-cells-and-genes_b_9516176.

2. Before you go mental at this claim, read further. I am not
saying that we have a choice to hurt when we break our
leg or a choice to be happy when we lose a loved one.
I'm saying that, all our lives, we have been fed a way
of perceiving our dukkha. It has become our way of
living, of reacting, of responding to circumstances. But
circumstances are not just created in the moment they
occur. They are choices we make across our entire lives—
choosing beliefs, choosing to feel certain things and not
others, choosing our attitudes and thoughts, etc. These
are choices that we make or don't make. In the end, this
fashions our reactions to events. Even physical pain can
be controlled with the mind, if we learn to do so. And

the choice to learn this technique is merely one step in the process of becoming skilled at it. It takes time. This is why I say all suffering is a choice. And, in the same way that the choices we make today can take years to have an effect through new skills, the choice we didn't make to learn something, years ago, can result in more pain tomorrow, because we don't know how to handle it better at that time. Some will call this victim blaming, but again, read further and you will see that there is no dispassion in my reflection on this matter. Indeed, quite the opposite. The most loving we can ever be to another person is to demonstrate to them the means of taking responsibility and removing suffering from their lives. In the meantime, we all help to deal with suffering using the best tools we have. Like an accident in the kitchen—sometimes you get a mop and help clean up. Afterwards, let's talk about preventing the accident from occurring again.

Chapter 5: Our Spiritual Heritage

1. Buddhadasa Bhikkhu. Dhammic Socialism. p67. Thai Inter-Religious Commission for Development, Bangkok. 1993 (2nd edition). Translated by Donald K. Swearer.
2. The Vedas. World History. [Internet]. [Cited December 19, 2021]. Available from: https://www.worldhistory.org/The_Vedas/.
3. Genesis 3:5 KJV (King James Version).
4. Luke 17:21 KJV.

Chapter 6: From Free Spirituality to Organized Religion

1. Lee, R.B., Daly, R. (eds). The Cambridge Encyclopedia of Hunters and Gatherers. pp411–418. Cambridge University Press. 2005.
2. These 16 include: Bahais, Buddhists, Chinese folk-religionists, Christians, Confucianists, Daoists,

Ethnoreligionists, Hindus, Jains, Jews, Muslims, New Religionists, Shintoists, Sikhs, Spiritists, Zoroastrians.

3. The Global Religious Landscape. December 18, 2012. Pew Research Institute. [Internet]. [Cited February 2, 2022]. Available from: https://www.pewforum.org/2012/12/18/global-religious-landscape-exec/.

4. Guillen, R. The Vatican's Finances. 1994.

5. How Much Gold Does the Catholic Church Own? March 27, 2015. goldrefiners.com. [Internet]. [Cited December 28, 2021]. Available from: http://www.goldrefiners.com/blog/2015/3/27/how-much-gold-does-the-catholic-church-own.

6. Buddhadasa Bhikkhu. Dhammic Socialism. p67. Thai Inter-Religious Commission for Development, Bangkok. 1993 (2nd edition). Translated by Donald K. Swearer.

7. I was reading even today that, under investigation by French authorities, France's Catholic Church was found to have had at least 2500 child molesters as priests since the 1950s. But this is just the tip of the iceberg. No religions have been spared this rot because they all rely upon hierarchy that is easily corrupted over the centuries. The full story is available at: https://www.reuters.com/world/europe/french-catholic-church-had-estimated-3000-paedophiles-since-1950s-commission-2021-10-03/.

8. Buddhadasa Bhikkhu. Dhammic Socialism. p46. Thai Inter-Religious Commission for Development, Bangkok. 1993 (2nd edition). Translated by Donald K. Swearer.

Chapter 7: The Three Marks of Existence

1. Buddhadasa Bhikkhu. Dhammic Socialism. p47. Thai Inter-Religious Commission for Development, Bangkok. 1993 (2nd edition). Translated by Donald K. Swearer.

2. Ajarn Brahm. Opening the Door to Your Heart. p153. Buddhist Publication Society Inc. 2006.

Chapter 8: Defilements

1. Buddhadasa Bhikkhu. Dhammic Socialism. p83. Thai Inter-Religious Commission for Development, Bangkok. 1993 (2nd edition). Translated by Donald K. Swearer.

2. In my book *Provolution*, I included an entire chapter on this phenomenon, so I won't repeat my conclusions here. However, in summary, Dr. Candace Pert wrote about the "Molecule of Emotion" in her eponymous book, after being a part of the team that discovered the receptor for peptides in the 1990s. Her remarkable work detailed how, each time emotions are felt, there is a corresponding release of peptides into the body, and these peptides congregate around organs and tissue. Moreover, the peptides are released from glands located in similar positions to the Indian Chakra system. Plus, different peptides were released for each emotion and aggregated in different places, corresponding to the spiritual idea that bodily organs and parts each have an emotional representation (the heart = love; the kidneys = fear etc.) However, the most shocking fact she discovered was that the aggregation of these peptides, over time, is linked to serious health issues. This implied that bodily disease, in some cases, is directly a product of mental creation, just as spiritual disciplines have been saying for thousands of years.

3. Adair, C. 9 Most Addicting Games in the World. [Internet]. [Cited January 3, 2022]. Available from: https://gamequitters.com/most-addicting-games/.

4. Buddhadasa Bhikkhu. Handbook for Mankind. p23. Dhammasapa Books. 1990.

Chapter 9: The Illusion of Progress

1. Buddhadasa Bhikkhu. Dhammic Socialism. p72. Thai Inter-Religious Commission for Development, Bangkok. 1993 (2nd edition). Translated by Donald K. Swearer.

2. During research into this chapter, I looked through numerous educational websites on prehistoric tribal life and found many sites using this kind of adjective as a fair description of society in prehistoric times. While it is impossible to say exactly what life was like, as the gift society suggests, there is evidence to paint a very different picture.

3. It is also noteworthy that, while ordinary people can see the charity in donating food they cannot eat, it has a rather more negative social impact. For example, the EU wastes 89.2 million tons of food each year, but were that gifted to a poorer economy, it would have a dire economic effect on the local food industry. In other words, even some forms of charity are harmful to the way CLD works. Monetary exchange has become so crucial to the way of life, that CLD values waste and inefficiency over charity and compassion.

4. Heinberg R. #215: Economic History in 10 Minutes. April 2010. [Internet]. [Cited March 26, 2022]. Available from: http://richardheinberg.com/215-economic-history-in-10-minutes.

5. Luke 18:22 KJV.

6. The 5 inner thieves we must avoid. Quoted from Guru Granth Sahib Ji, 676. [Internet]. [Cited March 26, 2022]. Available from: https://www.sikhismguide.net/five-forbidden-virtues/.

7. Qur'an. Surah Al-Humazah 104.1–6.

Chapter 10: Golden Ages and Enlightenment

1. Ferris J. How Humans Evolved Supersize Brains. November 10, 2015. Quanta Magazine. [Internet]. [Cited March 26, 2022]. Available from: https://www.quantamagazine.org/how-humans-evolved-supersize-brains-20151110/.

2. Kara-Yakoubian, M. Brains are getting smaller in modern humans. November 16, 2021. Psypost. [Internet]. [Cited

March 26, 2022]. Available from: https://www.psypost. org/2021/11/brains-are-getting-smaller-in-modern-humans-62124.

3. Aryabhata (476–550CE), the Indian mathematician and astronomer, postulated the heliocentric model of the solar system a thousand years before Copernicus in 1543CE.

Chapter 11: The Neolithic Revolution

1. Diamond, J. The Worst Mistake in the History of the Human Race. May 1, 1999. Discover Magazine. [Internet]. [Cited March 26, 2022]. Available from: https://www. discovermagazine.com/planet-earth/the-worst-mistake-in-the-history-of-the-human-race.
2. Ibid.
3. Ibid.
4. Ibid.
5. Ibid.
6. Ibid.

Chapter 12: Spiritual Wisdom versus Practical Truth

1. Dahlberg, F. Woman the Gatherer. Yale University Press. 2009.
2. Dyble, M., Salali, G.D., Chaudhary, N., Page, A., Smith, D., Thompson, J., et al. Sex Equality Can Explain the Unique Social Structure of Hunter-Gatherer Bands. Science. Volume 348, Issue 6236, May 15, 2015, pp796–798. [Internet]. [Cited March 26, 2022]. Available from: https://www.science.org/ doi/10.1126/science.aaa5139.
3. Fickling, D. Research shows first impressions really count. Guardian. August 23, 2006. [Internet]. [Cited April 9, 2022]. Available from: https://www. theguardian.com/science/2006/aug/23/usnews. internationalnews#:~:text=It%20takes%20only%20one%20 tenth,%2C%20in%20the%20US%2C%20said.

4.   Please note that male and female energy does not translate directly to imply male and female genders. Both sexes have both energies. However, it is fair to say that females generally exhibit more female energy and men generally exhibit more male energy. This is not merely nurtured into us by, for example, putting girls in dresses and boys in trousers. There is a natural genetic predisposition of males and females to certain preferences that society has, over thousands of years, recognized as being more female or male in type. For example, *Science Daily* reported that "Children as young as 9 months old prefer to play with toys specific to their own gender." My point here is not to define energies as gender-specific but to merely illustrate that society as a whole has created a mental imbalance towards one way of thinking and away from another. This thinking is reinforced by stereotypes, such as the idea that femininity is weak and masculinity is strong. It is not about the type of energy we use, but our intention in using it. Is our objective selfish or selfless? Will we be kind or mean? Energies are just tools. However, we also need to tap into tools that soften our aggression, address our emotional state, and feed our compassion. This is female energy in action, whether in action through a man or a woman. The energy is genderless.

5.   Reece, T. Beyond Halloween: Witches, devils, trials and executions. October 25, 2017. National Catholic Reporter. [Internet]. [Cited March 26, 2022]. Available from: https://www.ncronline.org/news/opinion/beyond-halloween-witches-devils-trials-and-executions.

6.   Goodare, J. The European Witch-Hunt. pp267, 268. Routledge. 2010.

Chapter 13: Enslavement by Stealth

1. Agriculture. Encyclopedia Britannica. [Internet]. [Cited March 26, 2022]. Available from: https://www.britannica.com/topic/slavery-sociology/Agriculture.

2. Slavery in the 21st Century. Wikipedia. [Cited March 26, 2022]. Available from: https://en.wikipedia.org/wiki/Slavery_in_the_21st_century.

Chapter 14: Law and Money

1. Brown J. Imagine a feudal country where 432 families own half the land. Welcome to Scotland. August 2, 2013. The Independent. [Internet]. [Cited March 26, 2022]. Available from: https://www.independent.co.uk/news/uk/politics/imagine-a-feudal-country-where-432-families-own-half-the-land-welcome-to-scotland-8742545.html.

2. The "double coincidence of wants" is a phrase coined by the British economist William Stanley Jevons. It describes how barter is only viable if two people possess different things, of the same value, at the same time. Due to seasonal ripening and the rapid spoilage of crops, barter was actually quite rare.

Chapter 15: We-Topia: You Have Control

1. Curtin, C. Fact or Fiction?: Living People Outnumber the Dead. March 1, 2007. Scientific American. [Internet]. [Cited March 26, 2022]. Available from: https://www.scientificamerican.com/article/fact-or-fiction-living-outnumber-dead/.

2. Buddhadasa Bhikkhu. Dhammic Socialism. p115. Thai Inter-Religious Commission for Development, Bangkok. 1993 (2nd edition). Translated by Donald K. Swearer.

O-BOOKS

SPIRITUALITY

O is a symbol of the world, of oneness and unity; this eye
represents knowledge and insight. We publish titles on general
spirituality and living a spiritual life. We aim to inform and help
you on your own journey in this life.
If you have enjoyed this book, why not tell other readers by
posting a review on your preferred book site?

Recent bestsellers from O-Books are:

Heart of Tantric Sex
Diana Richardson
Revealing Eastern secrets of deep love and intimacy to Western
couples.
Paperback: 978-1-90381-637-0 ebook: 978-1-84694-637-0

Crystal Prescriptions
The A-Z guide to over 1,200 symptoms and their healing crystals
Judy Hall
The first in the popular series of eight books, this handy little
guide is packed as tight as a pill-bottle with crystal remedies for
ailments.
Paperback: 978-1-90504-740-6 ebook: 978-1-84694-629-5

Your Simple Path
Find Happiness in every step
Ian Tucker
A guide to helping us reconnect with what is really important in
our lives.
Paperback: 978-1-78279-349-6 ebook: 978-1-78279-348-9

365 Days of Wisdom
Daily Messages To Inspire You Through The Year
Dadi Janki
Daily messages which cool the mind, warm the heart and guide
you along your journey.
Paperback: 978-1-84694-863-3 ebook: 978-1-84694-864-0

Body of Wisdom
Women's Spiritual Power and How it Serves
Hilary Hart
Bringing together the dreams and experiences of women across
the world with today's most visionary spiritual teachers.
Paperback: 978-1-78099-696-7 ebook: 978-1-78099-695-0

Dying to Be Free
From Enforced Secrecy to Near Death to True Transformation
Hannah Robinson
After an unexpected accident and near-death experience, Hannah
Robinson found herself radically transforming her life, while a
remarkable new insight altered her relationship with her father, a
practising Catholic priest.
Paperback: 978-1-78535-254-6 ebook: 978-1-78535-255-3

The Ecology of the Soul
A Manual of Peace, Power and Personal Growth for Real People
in the Real World
Aidan Walker
Balance your own inner Ecology of the Soul to regain your
natural state of peace, power and wellbeing.
Paperback: 978-1-78279-850-7 ebook: 978-1-78279-849-1

Not I, Not other than I
The Life and Teachings of Russel Williams
Steve Taylor, Russel Williams
The miraculous life and inspiring teachings of one of the World's
greatest living Sages.
Paperback: 978-1-78279-729-6 ebook: 978-1-78279-728-9

On the Other Side of Love
A woman's unconventional journey towards wisdom
Muriel Maufroy
When life has lost all meaning, what do you do?
Paperback: 978-1-78535-281-2 ebook: 978-1-78535-282-9

Practicing A Course In Miracles
A translation of the Workbook in plain language, with
mentor's notes
Elizabeth A. Cronkhite
The practical second and third volumes of The Plain-Language
A Course In Miracles.
Paperback: 978-1-84694-403-1 ebook: 978-1-78099-072-9

Quantum Bliss
The Quantum Mechanics of Happiness, Abundance, and Health
George S. Mentz
Quantum Bliss is the breakthrough summary of success and spirituality secrets that customers have been waiting for.
Paperback: 978-1-78535-203-4 ebook: 978-1-78535-204-1

The Upside Down Mountain
Mags MacKean
A must-read for anyone weary of chasing success and happiness – one woman's inspirational journey swapping the uphill slog for the downhill slope.
Paperback: 978-1-78535-171-6 ebook: 978-1-78535-172-3

Your Personal Tuning Fork
The Endocrine System
Deborah Bates
Discover your body's health secret, the endocrine system, and 'twang' your way to sustainable health!
Paperback: 978-1-84694-503-8 ebook: 978-1-78099-697-4

Readers of ebooks can buy or view any of these bestsellers by clicking on the live link in the title. Most titles are published in paperback and as an ebook. Paperbacks are available in traditional bookshops. Both print and ebook formats are available online.
Find more titles and sign up to our readers' newsletter at http://www.johnhuntpublishing.com/mind-body-spirit
Follow us on Facebook at https://www.facebook.com/OBooks/
and Twitter at https://twitter.com/obooks